Financial Purity

Jessica V. Psalidas

INFINITY
PUBLISHING.COM

ISBN 0-7414-5316-9

Published by:
INFINITY
PUBLISHING.COM
1094 New DeHaven Street, Suite 100
West Conshohocken, PA 19428-2713
Info@buybooksontheweb.com
www.buybooksontheweb.com
Toll-free (877) BUY BOOK
Local Phone (610) 941-9999
Fax (610) 941-9959

Printed in the United States of America
Published March 2009

Thank you to the Almighty Lord for the gifts and love You give me. I cannot thank You or love You enough.

To William BC and Vera Watkins, thank you for all the time and effort you have dedicated to teach me and show me the basics of managing finances wisely. Your nuggets of gold have turned into much! I am grateful and deeply appreciate you!

To my father, who will not be able to see this book finished, but he will always remain a source of love, encouragement and support to me.

To Becky, Johanna, Jr. and Pericles, whom I love deeply, may we stay close always and may God smile upon you and keep you safe all the days of your lives.

Much love,

JVP

Table of Contents

Welcome

Do you ever wonder why you often find yourself with little or no money at all? Sometimes it can confuse and bewilder us to no end how week after week our money just goes to pay bills and we are left with very little or nothing to save, give, or to spend on anything but the necessities. This is a common problem for most people; whether they make a lot of money or a little makes no difference. Money is a funny thing: it can help us, but it cannot make us happy. I have known many wealthy people who still have no happiness. They are miserable, tense, and most certainly not happy at all. However, I have also known many wealthy people who are happy and at peace.

I am of the generation that got into debt at a young age; when I was still fairly young and in a low-wage bracket, I had an incredible amount of debt. I had no money, and I didn't enjoy my early twenties, as I should have, because I was always working trying to get out of debt. How I fell into debt will be discussed in more detail later in the book, and I will also describe certain actions I took over a period of time to get in debt as well as to get out of it.

During those young adult years I was not able to keep my finances pure and clean. Of course, I was not very knowledgeable about managing money, either. I was clueless to say the least. The only thing I knew about money was having a checking and a savings account. I had a credit card from a reputable bank and had $2000 in my savings account. I made $6.25 an hour, which that not much left after taxes, but I was young and still lived with my parents, so I thought I was rich! I probably would've been able to get rich had I managed my money better. I don't think my financial problems were only the result of the way I managed my money, however; the severe disobedience I had against God's orders also hurt me. I did not tithe, and I didn't do any charitable volunteering and giving from a pure nature that honored God. The only great thing I did was pay my credit card off in full, which lasted for a short period of time, but then I soon began using it again. After that, I had to pay the minimum monthly payment because I could not pay all of the balance off in one lump sum.

Having come from years of being in debt and having a poverty mentality, I will tell you my story in this book to show you how I got there and how I got out of it. I will give you recommendations and tools to help you not make the same decisions I made that got me in debt in the first place.

I would not say that falling into debt was a mistake, and I highly recommend that you do not call it a mistake either. Think God is not working in your life? Think again! Everything that happens to us is for a reason. Treat your reality as a learning curve. You need to change your vision and look at things differently.

This book is not a complicated book on investments (the kind that can sometimes be difficult to understand), but a simple, back-to-the-basics book on keeping your money pure and reserved for paying necessary bills and spending on godly activities.

Join me as I give you a fresh approach to financial purity. With the two of us working together, you will gain new vision and understanding of your finances, and you will be encouraged to build your own financial purity portfolio to help you stay focused on your vision and achieve your goals.

Warmly,

Jessica V. Psalidas

Financial

Purity

Chapter 1

Develop a Vision

Show me your ways, O LORD, teach me your paths. Psalm 25:4

Why develop a vision? If you were able to view your money portfolio from a height of 50,000 feet, what would you want it to look like? Would you like to have no debt? Have money in savings account? Be organized in handling your money? Would you want to simply have enough of it, including enough to give away? I believe everyone should develop a vision about their money, or in some cases, change their vision.

This book will provide an in-depth look at what we spend our money on, why we should stay away from certain things that waste our money, and why we need to have a vision about money. I think money – the use and management of it – is very important in our lives. Once you develop a vision, you will have a clear idea of what you want in life and what action you will need to take in order to get there.

What is your financial purity portfolio? Many people have heard of a financial portfolio, but what is a financial purity portfolio, and why is it different? As we discover the answer to that question we will examine money in a different light, in a simple way that allows us to be clear about the use and management of our money. We will go beyond what we have in savings and investments and look into some of our day to day spending habits and frequent purchases, as well as why we save, why we tithe, why we should have a will, and what can happen when we spend our money on wasteful vices. Most importantly, in this book I will encourage everyone to develop a financial vision for themselves and their family.

Having a vision gives you clarity as to what you want and what you need to do to get there. It gives purpose and focus to your money management and to the outlook you have concerning your money. Many people that I talk to about money have a grim view of it because they do not have enough of it on hand at any given time or they do not earn enough of it. I encourage you to have a positive, realistic outlook and attitude toward money for your own financial welfare. It does you no good to be irritated or upset about your financial status right now, because with a great attitude and determination, you can change your situation.

Developing a vision for your finances is the first step in building your financial purity portfolio. Utilizing and managing your money purely and cleanly, meaning spending your money on necessary and wholesome things, is one of the most important steps in developing your financial purity portfolio.

The first step I want you to take is to develop your financial vision by writing it down. If you are married, then develop your vision with your spouse. If you have children, include them too (at the level of their understanding based on their age). Chapter 9 will discuss why we should involve children in every aspect of financial management. If you are single, then determine your vision. The idea is to be clear on what you want your finances to look like. Be specific and honest.

Some people may think it is hard to focus on developing a vision due to their own difficult financial situation or, as some call it, the "financial crisis" we are experiencing in the U.S. at the time of this writing. If this describes you, please be encouraged! I would like to share with you some steps that I have implemented in my life to remain joyful and hopeful during any trying situation that comes along.

I refuse to let my morale get dragged down into the pits

Everyone seems to be in a state of panic over the financial situation in the U.S. economy, and it both saddens and frustrates me at the same time. We are, to a certain extent, part of the reason why our country is the way it is. When our morale goes down, so does everything else. We are gripped by fear over temporary difficulties that will soon pass. This country has experienced many challenging situations before, and we have always gotten through them. We will get through this too. We need to remain positive, encouraged, and stimulated to find new and exciting ways to spur our economic growth. We need to be stronger in prayer, which will keep our morale high. If we all lifted our spirits up higher and kept a positive attitude, we would experience a change for the better. Nothing good will come out of us being depressed, upset, angry, or fearful. These emotions will not get us ahead but rather will only hold us back. Stay in prayer and remain hopeful in God.

> *Cast all your anxiety on him because he cares for you. 1 Peter 5:7*

> *Have I not commanded? Be strong and courageous! Do not tremble or be dismayed, for the Lord your God is with you wherever you go. Joshua 1:9*

I am cautious of which news stations I watch

I believe it is important to watch the news so we are aware of what is going on in our beloved country, but some news networks tend to elaborate unnecessarily about issues to the point that they talk about them to death! Some local news stations focus on reporting extremely negative news using grim-faced reporters and anchors, and watching them regularly can either frighten or concern you.

These are the times when our emotions become frail and sensitive. Almost any negative report can rock our world for better or worse. Therefore, I stay away from those stations. I like to protect myself from negative people and negative commentaries that are only going to get me down. The news reports keep telling us, "It is only going to get worse!" I say, "It will only get better!" Tell yourself that too, and surround yourself with positive, jovial people.

I know this is not the first crisis we've endured

This is not the first time we have ever gone through a financial situation (or "crisis" as some may call it) in this nation. We will survive, and we will get through this. Do not corrupt your mind with negative thoughts such as, "Oh, no ... the world is falling apart!" Thinking this way will cause much devastation to your otherwise positive mindset, and it will keep your fears very much alive. On the contrary, you will be amazed at what can happen to your morale and your spirits when you remain positive, jovial, and at peace about the situation.

Because this is not the first time our country has experienced something like this, I know the situation will get better soon. *We* will get better. I believe that by changing our outlook, adjusting our lifestyles, and remaining positive, we will do a great service to those around us and to ourselves. Stay in prayer, remain spiritually strong, and most importantly, remain happy.

Let's not stop – let's move on

I have not changed my lifestyle at all. My bills are paid on time, I still go shopping, and I still enjoy life like I have always done. If we all stop, the world stops! We need to keep everything going and we need to learn to control our fears and survive. My friends and family know not to talk about the market or the financial situation with me. We keep it happy, surrounding ourselves with laughter, good food, and lots of jokes! No negativity is allowed.

These steps have done wonders for me as well as for those around me. So let's do a quick review of some morale-boosting tips:

- Don't let your morale go down into the pits

- Be careful of the news you watch
- Be careful who you speak to
- Do not let others' negativity bring you down
- Remember, this is not the first time; we will make it through this time just as we've always done.

I am not going to delve deep into the intricate and often complicated topics of investing and trading. We are going to talk about financial purity in a way that no other financial advocate has spoken to you before. This book contains simple yet effective practices that you can build into your everyday life, and by doing so, you will reap the benefits of the good seeds you've sown.

I even suggest that teens and college students adopt these good practices to get them disciplined and ready for their Financial Purity Portfolio. If you are in that age group, I am sure you are living life and enjoying it, but you can enjoy it even more when you're financially secure. That is not a difficult goal to reach when you adopt a system that is both simple and time saving. When you do so, you'll discover an additional benefit – that simplicity and saving time are excellent ways to save money.

Have you worked on developing your vision yet?

Come along with me as we dive into the details of every aspect of everyday life – things we all have to do and things we would rather not do. This system, which I have termed Financial Purity, will show you how to keep your money for its intended pure use and enjoyment; it will show you how organization is directly linked to saving money, what to not spend your money on; and by using this system you will discover that finding joy in simple, mundane things brings glory to God.

This is a whole new way to look at money. We tend to look at money from the standpoint of how much we have or how much we can save, but I have learned that money management involves much more than that. Of all the things in life, money seems to always be on the top of our priority list and for good reason.

It is the central part of our daily living, and having money is a necessity. I also believe it is a trial and test from God. I believe God trusts us with some kind of fortune, whether small or big, and it is up to us to manage it well. This is no small task, and sometimes it is no easy task, either, because we want to enjoy life and live it to the fullest as much as possible. There is nothing wrong with that – I am all for enjoying life and experiencing the best it has to offer, but I also know (and want to encourage everyone) that we must be organized, faithful to God's commands (a crucial step to having success), and make wise decisions. We will discuss what many people spend their money on and analyze whether it is beneficial to their financial well-being, physical well-being, or spiritual well-being.

I'm sure you have heard the time-honored saying that money does not buy happiness. That's true – it doesn't. It never will. However, proper money management and financial purity can bring you a peace of mind that eliminates stress and keeps you organized. To me, peace of mind is right up there with happiness.

The money we have, use, spend, and invest can say a lot about our financial purity as a whole. Don't assume because you are not a millionaire that you do not have to manage your money. *Au contraire*. In fact, because your finances might be limited, the need to manage your money wisely is even greater. I have heard people say time and time again, "Well, I am young and I don't make too much money, so what does it matter?" It matters a great deal! I cannot stress that enough. Handling your money wisely dictates whether you are wealthy or not, and wise or not. Another misconception people tend to have is that they don't need a will because they don't have a lot of money or a large estate. Nothing could be further from the truth. We will discuss this topic in chapter 10.

Have you worked on developing your vision yet? If so, CONGRATULATIONS! If not, let me encourage you to get BUSY!

Build your Life Plan

> *Plans succeed through good counsel; don't go to war without wise advice. Proverbs 12:15*

In addition to your vision, you should also have a Life Plan. Look at your financial purity portfolio as a plan to get you to where you want to be in your finances and, because finances are linked to everything, your life. Many people all around the world have not achieved their dreams because they never took the time to figure out what they wanted out of life. What do you want out of life? If you were writing your autobiography or memoirs, what would you want to be able to say you had accomplished in your lifetime? Because I value life, myself, and my parents, I need to make sure I make the best out of my life, because I will be here for a short period of time and I do not want to waste it. I am sure you feel the same way.

Accomplishments are the order of the day in my life; this is why I have a life plan, a plan that states that before I pass on to Heaven, I will have achieved XYZ. Will I achieve all my goals? Maybe ... maybe not! But I will never know until I decide what my calling may be or what I can offer the world and then make a plan to fulfill that calling.

Realistically, you do not need to be extremely wealthy to achieve your goals; however, you *do* need to be organized just to have the freedom to not have to deal with financial issues that take up your time or cost you additional (and unnecessary) money. For example, forgetting to pay a bill can cause you to have to pay a late fee; it can cause you to have to make an extra phone call, which wastes your time (and time is money); furthermore, a late payment forces you to deal with the extra paperwork involved in receiving late notices. A good organized plan can help you not forget to pay the bill, thus saving you from paying that extra fee. We will discuss this at length later on in the book.

If you are in a position of financial privilege, then God bless you! I am sure that even though you are wealthy, you can still build a strong Financial Purity Portfolio, which is all about using your finances for godly pursuits and godly actions.

I do want to touch on the importance of having a plan in place for the long-term well-being of your financial purity. While many people cringe when they're asked about having a plan, it is very important to your financial well-being. Many people go through life never having a plan; their goal is to simply enjoy life, but usually they hinder their ability to do so because they're always struggling with their finances. You can choose to determine what you want to happen in your life or you can choose to just live life every day, one day at a time, and see what happens. The choice is yours, but no matter what path you take, I still think you should have a Financial Purity Portfolio and a vision for your future whether you have a Life Plan or not.

The two biggest challenges in life are relationships and finances. I was once asked what I would do if I was in a position of decision-making, power, or influence in the school system. I replied that I would add classes on finances and relationship building as early as the third grade, and I would have the instruction in these classes build from one year to the next all through high school. I would also incorporate these classes into the early college curriculum as "non-elective" courses.

Throughout life we all have to deal with money and other people no matter where we go, where we live, or what we do for a living. It is simply unavoidable. Because the school system does not have as part of their curriculum training in money management and building successful relationships, everyone is left to struggle on their own in these two vital aspects of living a happy and full life.

No matter what career you choose, you will need to manage your money for the rest of your life. You will need to work with people and have good manners for the rest of your life.

We clearly need to increase our knowledge of how to handle money and relationships. We need to learn how to get along better with people, and how to manage our money so that we do not end up in bankruptcy. While I cannot add classes in these topics to the school curriculum, I can write this book in an attempt to help those who read it understand some basic concepts about money management.

We cannot be wishful thinkers, but instead we must be people who will take action and make things happen in our lives. That is why I want to motivate, encourage, and teach you through this book. The topic that Jesus taught the most about in the New Testament was money. Over one-third of His teachings were about money, so it must be important.

Because money can be a tricky thing and many people struggle with the management of their financial affairs, I am going to ask you to please change your vision and get a new vision concerning money, what it means to you, and how you manage it. Whatever notions and concepts you might have, I would like you to re-think what you know about money and how you manage your financial affairs. I am going to teach you how to build a financial purity portfolio, and all throughout this book we will go over the details of what that will look like.

We will look into credit card management, budgeting, vices we waste our money on, and the long-term spiritual effects vices can have on us. We will also examine the importance of having a life plan, a plan for most anything, and how this can lead to wise money management both short-term and long-term. We will also take a look at how good, clear organization leads to a fuss-free day and wise money habits, and therefore it *does* contribute to better financial management.

All this is money management at its finest. Will it ever be perfect? No. Will it ever be exactly the way we want it to be? Perhaps, but we have to develop it and work at it. We have to be intentional in our financial planning and money management like we are when we get dressed in the morning and go to work or when we do something special. Treat your finances as something special, something dear to you. Find the balance between good money management and not being too attached to money from a spiritual perspective. Money management takes work, it takes effort, and sometimes it simply takes experience.

When you make a dedicated effort and you understand what works for your family and what doesn't, you will become experienced at handling your finances and you will get good at it. You will then become (or work toward being) debt-free depending on where you are in your financial life. Our finances are like a living being, and we can develop them to be strong or not. It depends on how much effort we put into managing them.

Some people want so much to be wealthy, and yet they spend every dime when they get their paycheck. At this rate, becoming wealthy may not happen for quite some time.

Another thing I want to mention is that every person or family has their own unique definition of what it means to be wealthy. I am not saying that being wealthy is having any amount of money in the bank, because some people consider being debt-free as wealthy. Good for them! A debt-free lifestyle can be very liberating and mean all the wealth in the world to some people. It is different for everyone. That is why when you develop your vision concerning *your* finances, you can decide what wealth means to you. Make it personal; determine what is meaningful to you, and then develop your plan based on the concepts in this book.

Managing and understanding your finances is a life-long process. I don't think you ever "arrive" at the finish line or ever stop studying new ways to manage your money.

God wants us to use our money for godly actions and intentions, as well as to manage and use it for our daily living. While God allows us to manage our money on our own, He says it is a blessing to use it for godly action and godly intentions. Avoiding wasting our money on vices is a blessing too, and can help maintain our financial purity.

Let's recap what we've discussed, what we need to do, and what we will soon complete ...

- Develop your vision ...what we've discussed
- Create your Life Plan ... what we need to do
- Build your financial purity portfolio ... what we will soon complete

Change your vision and make your plans. This is a big part of your financial purity portfolio so you can budget and plan your money management for your dreams and that of your family.

Chapter 2

Organization and Planning

Good planning and hard work lead to prosperity, but hasty shortcuts lead to poverty. Proverbs 21:5

Organization and planning have a direct correlation to saving time and money. In this chapter I will go over some easy steps that will help you develop healthy habits of organization and planning. You may think that making plans and to-do lists take up time and are very difficult to implement. However, the busier your schedule the more important planning and organization is to your day. The simpler your schedule, the easier it is to incorporate planning and organization into your day.

Organization and planning are very important to your financial purity portfolio. For example, keeping an organized shopping list can keep you from spending an extra $50 or $100 on items you do not need. Cutting coupons, keeping them organized, and taking them with you when you go grocery shopping can help you save money at checkout time. Organizing your week in a way that distributes the household chores can help you save money because you find that you actually do have time to do your own housecleaning, and therefore you don't really need to hire a cleaning company. Organizing your week can help you remember important appointments like visiting customers, attending meetings, going to the dentist or taking your pet to the vet.

On the other hand, forgetting even the little but very important things you need to get done can cause you to have to make extra phone calls, which waste time, when you could have saved yourself time by following your list and not forgetting. Calendars work wonders, to-do lists have power, and plans give us focus to make it all happen.

An organized method

The first steps to take in accomplishing anything are organizing and planning. I have learned this from observing individual people and families I know who have accomplished many goals, projects, dreams, and much, much more. Every time I take a close look at their lives I get so inspired and see that anything can be done! So what is an organized method? Organizing means writing down what you have in the bank, the money you need to earn (considered on a weekly basis), the items you need to purchase, and an inventory of all the belongings you have in your home.

Next, you need to map out your weekly schedule including work and home tasks, shopping, and events you plan to attend with your family and/or friends (or any other activities you have going on in your life). When all this is written down – your financial inventory and your daily/weekly schedule – things will start to get clearer for you because you will have a visual map of your daily life.

Be specific and include ALL the tasks you do – even putting gas into the car or getting the car cleaned. On that note, putting gas into the car could be done on a Saturday; this way nothing interferes with the precious weekday time you need to give to your family. Of course, if you need to put gas into your car during the week, then do it. The most important point is to maintain a structured, organized method to your week that optimizes cost control and maximizes family time.

Many parents put a high value on the time they can spend with their children, and rightly so. Family is so precious, and everything you do, even planning, is for your children's welfare and wellbeing.

Take your time when making your inventory list. Go to a coffee shop, and sit down with a coffee or tea and make your list. If you are married, sit down with your spouse and do the list together. Address every issue you can think of, and be enthusiastic as you make the list; in doing so everything will flow naturally and you will not forget tasks no matter how menial you think they are. Take pride and joy in accomplishing this important first step, but most of all, add love to this exercise.

We are all very sophisticated people; we are very capable of multi-tasking at every turn, and with a good plan and organization all can be achieved smoothly and flawlessly.

Many people are fascinated with Buckingham Palace because of its beauty, magnificence, and the longstanding power of the British monarchy that it represents. If we were to take a look behind the closed doors at the running and management of this amazing living and working place, we would be amazed.

The planning and management that go into keeping it running are quite amazing. Every aspect of the place has a manager and a management plan that rivals none other except perhaps the military and the White House.

The management and implementation of assigned tasks are begun as early as 5:00–6:00 am, quietly and carefully, but most importantly, with a plan. Everyone knows their role from the time they begin their workday to the time it ends; they know what they need in order to accomplish their tasks, how they are going to get them done, where they will work for the day, and what their expected results are. It is stunning and incredible the effort and time that goes into keeping the palace running impeccably every day. But, that is what it takes.

It takes work and energy to keep things running well and on time. The endeavors that the palace and military put into their everyday activities, is something similar to what we are going to do in our everyday lives. Take heart, pride, and joy! I am not trying to bring arrogance into the picture, but God's Word says we are to put our heart into our work and let the fruits of our efforts shine – even if our work simply involves making windows shine! Yes, be happy as you do your household chores. Taking good care of your home and your possessions will make them last longer. Your money will thank you and God will be glorified! After all, God blessed you with what you have.

The purpose of this book is not to tell you that you can't enjoy your hard-earned money; it is to teach you how to do it carefully and wisely. Making organization and planning a priority as well as a regular part of your life will help you every day.

Have you ever looked at your busy schedule and wondered how you're going to get something important done, especially when you already have a million things to do? If so, I know the feeling; I've been there! Many times I've wondered how on earth was I going to get everything done! Whenever I would feel overwhelmed by this thought, I would get inspired by godly women who *do* manage to get everything done, and I would also consider those in the military who get everything done and who execute their plans quite flawlessly.

It all comes down to planning, planning, and more planning. Planning then turns into goal setting and task layout. It is amazing to see how someone this organized does it, but instead of just being amazed, I simply followed in their footsteps and took their advice. There were several steps they took when getting their tasks organized; I will share with you what they did, which is also what I do, and how it all comes together.

Planning is so effective that you will be able to keep the house clean and organized, get the laundry done in a way that it is under control and your energy bill is also under control, dinner gets done every night and is healthy, bills are paid on time, car maintenance is fulfilled on time, work goals are accomplished, food shopping is done in a timely manner and without too much stress, family time is accomplished, fun time with the family is scheduled, and you have time for yourself whether it be with friends or just having a simple quite time.

With flawless planning and advance thinking, you can have everything under control; your finances will be in order, and you will have peace.

Many have adopted this proven method and as a result they spend less time fretting and more time getting things done. If you are determined to get your finances in order and have a life that is under control, take charge and join me as we take a look at an organization method that has proven time and time again to do just that!

Ever wonder how CEOs, presidents, and high-profile managers have time to do everything? Good planning! Yes, they might have managers and personal assistants, but they all institute, manage, and follow some type of plan. If you could ask highly successful people how they do it, they would most likely tell you they manage their boss's schedule and their own work schedule, plus their personal one – which makes three schedules they have to manage. They *have* to be organized and efficient in all they do.

How is this important to financial purity? It is very important. You cannot expect to have total control over your finances, including taking care of your needs and tracking your spending habits, until you make a total inventory of everything you do, need, and want. Most of us are visual learners, and once we see everything mapped out it makes it easier to plan and manage our money better. Many people follow this discipline yearly, quarterly, and monthly, and some do it weekly. Weekly planners are very organized people who have a minimal amount of chaos in their life because their organization helps them deal with unforeseen events much better since they're already managing the foreseen, planned events. Their stress levels are lower and their sanity is somewhat protected, and they tend to get a lot accomplished.

If you have children, I definitely recommend that you get into the habit of planning yours and your kids' schedules on a weekly basis. Having kids is wonderful, but they can bring chaos into your home if you aren't in control of your life and theirs; having an organization plan is a sure way to make sure their plans are in effect and the plans that you and your spouse have are fulfilled as well. This will tell your children that you care enough about them to ensure that no one forgets their activities, school events, or sports events. They will love you for it because it makes them feel important. Kids need to feel a sense of purpose and belonging, and having an organized plan for their lives simply means you are determined to make sure you are there for them when they need you and that you do not forget about what's important to them.

Let's take a look at what needs organization and what needs planning. I think that everything we do needs planning and organization. From our sock drawer to our biggest dreams, they can all benefit from a healthy dose of planning and organization. Don't get tired and grow weary; put effort into your life, and choose to really *live* life every day! You'll discover that once you build a system that you are comfortable with, it will be easy to maintain it.

What needs to be organized and planned? Almost anything you need to manage in your life. A typical list might look something like this, and we will look into each one in more detail:

- Getting organized for better planning
- Work, work goals, meetings and appoint-

ments

- Paying the bills
- Shopping for clothing and household items
- Grocery shopping
- Dinner and food preparation
- Laundry
- Housecleaning
- House maintenance, lawn care, and repairs
- Car maintenance, including putting gas in the car
- Personal growth planning, including kids
- Church and related activities
- Entertainment planning
- Vacation planning
- Mentoring and coaching planning
- Unexpected events planning
- Estate planning – saving and planning

This list is in no particular order of priority. You can create your own list and prioritize it in a way that suits the unique needs of your life and your family's. Let's take a look at how a particular area might be planned out. Again, this might be slightly different for everyone. Develop what works for you and what can save you time and money.

Getting organized for better planning

A method that has worked for me is to create a to-do list for every day. I have a day in the week where I take from about 30 minutes to an hour to plan my week. This includes planning for all the tasks that need to be completed each day.

This will ensure that you have given thought to everything that needs to be accomplished every day of the week –you will even have your grocery list already made for a quick trip to the supermarket. Include all appointments for visits at work, to the doctor, dentist, veterinarian, or any car maintenance that needs to be done. This ensures that you will not forget anything.

Here is an inside look at what my weekly plan looks like on a daily basis:

- Monday – Wrestling night
- Tuesday – bill paying night

- Wednesday – laundry day
- Thursday – housecleaning day
- Friday – movie night or a fun night
- Saturday – errand day
- Sunday – Sabbath day, church, and relax

Yearly goals are established two months before the year's end. Quarterly goals are done before the first two weeks of the new year. Weekly goals are done every Saturday and modified only if necessary, such as if a sudden and necessary change in plans comes along.

I evaluate my goals weekly to check on my progress in fulfilling them. Will every goal be accomplished? Perhaps and perhaps not. One year I had over fifty-three goals to meet – actually, I think it was fifty-five, and of those, there were only about five goals I was unable to accomplish. I can tell you that moving forward in my life I will not exceed twenty goals in any given year. Let me explain why.

By the time the third quarter of the year had come around, I was exhausted to the point where I needed medical help. I hated that. I had been so certain that because I had this awesome plan and high levels of energy I would be able to accomplish all my goals, but that was not the case. When I had fully recuperated from total exhaustion, I realized what I was not capable of doing and what I needed to avoid, and then I avoided it. Fifty-three goals in a year is something I will not try to do again! Some suggest only five goals a year, but depending on your circumstances, you might be able to accomplish more – just try not to do too much. You do not want to wear yourself out, but you do want to make sure you are accomplishing your dreams and fulfilling you life plan. If you don't have a life plan yet, don't worry – we will discuss later in the book how to create one.

I think everyone should have a life plan, which is a plan that maps out what you want to accomplish in your lifetime. What do you want people to remember you for? Is it being an AWESOME parent? A fantastic employee? A memorable soldier? Whatever it is, be clear about it so that you can make it happen. The best way to do that is to have a life plan.

Find a place where you are inspired to think and reflect on what you want your life to look like. Write it down and make some of your yearly goals based on your life plan. Many people who do have a life plan achieve their ultimate mission and life vision statement, and this is due in large part to having written it down.

Part of my life plan includes 101 things I want to do before I die. Every year I try to chalk off a couple of them and go on to the next ones. I love it! Every time I chalk them off I feel like I have climbed Mount Everest. I cannot explain why, but accomplishing things I want to do before I pass away makes me happy. One of my life goals was to get out of debt, and when I did, I felt like King Kong!

I also celebrated this milestone with a beautiful necklace, which was my reward for having achieved it. I normally do not reward myself for accomplishing goals, but becoming debt-free was a big deal and a huge part of my own financial purity. Not only did I reward myself with a beautiful necklace, but I also had a small party with champagne to celebrate. It was that big a deal to me. Perhaps you have a big life goal you want to make happen and when you do accomplish it, you want to celebrate the achievement. You will never know that feeling of accomplishment until you clarify what you want to do and how you plan to make that happen.

Now, let's take a deeper look into the different things that fill our everyday lives and see how we can make a plan for getting them done.

Paying the bills

This is a very important task, and one that we should love to take care of. I know, that seems like an unusual thing to say; not many people like paying their bills because it seems that all their hard-earned money goes straight toward paying the bills. But that's an integral part of why we work – to earn a living so that we can pay the bills. It's something we all have to get used to, and actually we can learn to love it if we approach bill paying with the right mindset. To keep some organization in fulfilling this responsibility, I recommend you pick a day in the week to pay your bills. A better thing to do is see about having all your bills' due dates fall within the same week, especially if you have bills that are due sporadically all throughout the month.

I've found it works best to choose the second or third week of the month so there's enough money to pay all the bills.

When you call to find out if you can change the due date to a specific date, explain what you are doing; most companies can accommodate your request. If not, then set aside a specific day of each week to pay your bills routinely and on time. Memorize each bill's approximate due date, but notate the exact due dates on a calendar when each bill arrives. Then when you sit down on the day of each week that you've designated as bill-paying day, make payments on the bills whose due dates haven't come and gone yet. Every week, know this is the day you pay the upcoming bills. Do not schedule anything during this time and do not make any exceptions. Pay your bills – it is all part of your financial purity, utilizing your money to pay your bills and to pay them on time. When you use your hard-earned money to pay the bills in an organized manner you are showing one of the true purposes of your money.

Make sure you always have enough stamps, envelopes, checks, and pens on hand to do the job unless you pay your bills online. However, if some of your bills cannot be paid online, make sure you are prepared with all the necessary items to do the job at hand with dedication and love – to get your bills paid on time in a regular fashion.

I love paying the bills. It feels so good to be able to pay them! Pick a day in the week to do this and make it happen.

Let's recap...

- Pick a day in the week to pay your bills
- Try to have all your bills be due on the same date
- Follow your plan to ensure that no bill is late
- Remember, when bills are paid on time, you are not billed late fees.

Shopping for clothing and household items

By no means do we have to destroy our budget or look like we are dressing from another generation just to be able to dress stylishly and afford doing so. Here are some guidelines for shopping for clothes;

these have worked for me, and I think perhaps this method can work for you.

I normally go shopping (for clothes, shoes, purses, etc.) about three times a year. These are very specific times of the year when I shop to help me be and look the best I can and most importantly, to save money while doing it. I go shopping in the beginning of the year in January to get me ready for the cool weather and the colors of the season. I buy pants, shirts, shoes, purses, and accessories if I need them. Because I have bought some accessories in the past, I may not have to buy any more – the ones I have may go well with the new outfits I buy. I tend to buy items that can be mixed and matched. So depending on my current inventory, which I have checked in advance, I may or may not buy anything new.

I go shopping again right before summer to make sure I have cool and hip clothing I can wear all during the summer. I also make sure that the colors are in season and that I will be comfortable in any location I may go to. Then I go shopping at the beginning of the holiday season to be ready for the parties and all the good celebrations from

Thanksgiving through New Year's Eve. These are the three times of the year when I go shopping.

I also purge my closet once a year. Anything that I have not worn for an entire year I take out of my closet and give to a charity.

Every time I go shopping I make sure I've set a budget for myself and that I stick to it. The budgeted amount varies depending on how much I was able to save during the months since the last time I shopped and how much clothing I will need to purchase in the new shopping trip. Some pieces of clothing are classic styles that can be worn at any time, like a good pair of black pants, for example. So depending on what I truly need, that is what I purchase.

I also carve out a couple of days in my schedule to make sure I get the job done right. I take a day to research through the latest fashion magazines, and then I take two days to buy everything that I will need, making sure I go to the stores that carry my size and have affordable prices. Sometimes, it takes longer than two days, and that is okay. I normally carve out about three to four days for this process either straight together or over two weekends. I then take some time to organize my closet by color; this way I always know what I have and thus I don't get confused thinking I have to run out and buy a pink blouse, for example, when I already have one.

I also organize my accessories by color. I keep them in a special clear hanging container that allows me to organize everything by color, and I hang this in my closet. This way I can take my hanging container and lay it up against the outfit I've chosen for the day and see what looks good with the outfit. It also helps me to not buy accessories I already have, thus saving me valuable money. True, there may be something I just want to buy because I think it is beautiful, and I know it can go with one of my outfits and I just simply want it. If that happens (which is more often than not), I consider three things before making the purchase: if I can afford it, if I have enough money in my overall budget for this extra expense, and if it will not cause clutter in my closet. I get overwhelmed with clutter, and I am careful to not buy too much too unnecessarily. I tend to like beautiful things, and when I go shopping I always find a way to justify why I should buy something even if I don't need it. When this happens I take a moment to reason with myself and remind myself why I should not buy it. Also, before I go shopping, I always pray and ask the Lord to help me stay in check!

Following a method such as this makes you aware of every purchase you make and helps keep you from running out to buy something you think you do not have. Setting aside specific times of the year to make big shopping trips helps you not fall into the spending trap of randomly wandering the mall and making impulse purchases simply because you're there. When you use a disciplined approach, you're still able to buy what you need – you just buy intelligently. Less is best – buy wisely. You will save money and you'll still look great too! Having a plan for your shopping experiences will help you control your money and your habits. Start by taking small steps until you can adapt to a system that works best for you.

If you're like me you enjoy buying books, and you like to browse through the bookstore with a cup of coffee. But when time is limited and you must have a book, shop online. Most major bookstores have a website as well. You can easily have the book purchased in a matter of minutes without leaving your home. How cool is that? You can also do gift and holiday shopping online too. This is my favorite because I can save time on finding parking in an extremely crowded parking lot at the mall; I avoid unnecessary spending due to sales and clearance racks; I avoid the frustration of hustling and bustling through the crowds at the mall. All of this takes time away from other things you can be doing and remember, that old saying "Time is money" is true.

Online shopping for the holidays is the way to go unless you are very organized and have purchased all your gifts a couple of months in advance, which if you have, I applaud you. You have contributed greatly to your financial purity and to some degree to your health. I have seen many people lose their control over a long line, a parking space they've just got to have, and other silly things that do not matter in the grand scheme of things. If this is something you have a hard time coping with, consider the alternative of online shopping. Here is a breakdown of some things you can avoid by shopping online in the comfort of your home:

- Time wasted looking for parking
- Time wasted standing in long lines to pay for something
- Possibility of spending excess money due to a sale that catches your eye
- Frustrations later on standing in long lines to do returns

We can go on with the list, but I think you can get the idea. While there are many people that truly enjoy shopping as a Holiday blissful event, others aren't so lucky to feel that way. I have seen many fights break out in the parking lot over a parking spot, forget the insides of the mall. I rather do online shopping to avoid all the commotion, to save me time. What will take hours on end at the mall to accomplish will take maybe thirty minutes online, I opt for the online experience. Just the thought of saving all that time and the stress is a big motivator for me. This is part of my financial purity.

I do go to the mall, but not during the busy Holiday season. Forget it. I just do not have enough time to do it. I almost have to buy online.

Many people go in to the mall and come out with triple of what they originally expected to buy. This does not help you save money, regardless if you needed the items anyway. You could have bought the same thing at another time when the plan was in order to do it then when the budget was reserved for it.

Let's recap...

- Make a good shopping plan
- Make shopping an event with goals in mind
- Take inventory of what you have in your closet before you shop
- Do not over buy or buy double
- Buy accessories that go with most of your outfits
- Avoid shopping just because there are sales going on
- If you are limited on time, opt for the online shopping experience

Grocery Shopping

Plan regular trips to the grocery store, with a well-thought-out recipe plan, and a dedicated amount of time for shopping. This allows you to comparison shop for the best price and to read the labels to avoid unhealthy ingredients such as too much fat, sodium, sugar, or high-fructose corn syrup. When you make a trip to the grocery store, don't forget your shopping list; this way when you're ready to prepare your meals during the week for you and your family, you'll have all the ingredients you need. Divide your list into sections – dairy, vegetables, meats, and so on. Write your list in the order of the layout of the store so that you'll only go up and down each aisle once, thus saving time. This method, along with having your list in hand, will prevent you from overspending in any way. Having a list helps you stay focused and get in and out of the store in a jiffy. You already know what you want and need, and therefore you don't have to linger or wander aimlessly down the aisles.

Sometimes you end up buying what you don't need or you forget to buy the one thing you *do* need resulting in an extra trip to the grocery store, which then cuts into your time and gas. See how important having a list is? You save time and money – financial purity.

When planning your weekly menus, have your family weigh in to find out what they would like to eat, then write it out and create a menu just like if you were at a restaurant. Get creative and make it fun! Your family will be excited and intrigued to see what you are going to offer them. Be sure to include dessert – this will keep your family wanting to eat at home rather than wanting to go out to a restaurant where they can get dessert – which normally racks up the bill!

Pull out your cookbooks and breeze through the recipes; see what they have to offer that your family would like. Pay attention to the dessert menu, too; there are many desserts you can make in a jiffy and they're healthy, too!

Now, make a list of the ingredients necessary to produce your menu for the week. Go shopping with your menu and ingredients list in hand. Go to the stores that you know will have the ingredients you are looking for and remember to buy everything in one fell swoop, which will save you gas, money, and time.

If seasoned meats are on your menu, season them when you get home and store them in zip-lock freezer bags and label them accordingly: Monday night's dinner, Tuesday's dinner, and so on. Each morning when you leave to go to work, take out the meat so it is completely thawed out when you get home from work. That way, by the time you get home you have seasoned, thawed-out meat ready to cook for your family.

Everyone loves to eat out once in a while. Some like to eat out all the time due to their work schedule and their distaste for cooking. With today's hectic schedules and busy lives, the art of cooking is almost non-existent, but eating out also costs much more money than cooking dinner and eating at home. Eating out also has a negative effect on our health. There is no comparison to home cooking. Don't like to cook? Short on time? No worries, tune in to the Food Network, where they can show you how to cook healthy meals in no time at all. Don't have time to watch your shows? Then buy an easy-to-read and easy-to-follow cookbook that shows you how to cook well without spending a great deal of time doing it. There really is no secret to it; all it takes is good planning and good execution.

Enjoy eating out once in a while! Everyone loves eating out for a special occasion or for a change from the routine ... just don't make it an everyday habit. Make a menu of what you will be cooking for the entire week – yes Monday through –Sunday, and then shop according to that menu. You'll find that once you have all the ingredients in your kitchen for making good meals, you'll prefer to eat at home more than eating out.

Still not convinced eating at home together is a good idea?

- Studies have shown that eating together as a family helps children make wiser decisions, such as staying away from smoking and drinking.
- Eating together makes for great conversations, which helps you stay involved in your family's life.

- Eating together brings unity and awareness in the family.
- Cooking at home saves you hundreds of dollars a month.
- Cooking at home helps you and your children stay healthy and avoid obesity. Items like fried foods and pizza do no good to a growing, vulnerable young body.
- Kids love when their parents cook for them – and they especially like to have their friends over for a meal with their family.
- You can be confident that you are spending your money wisely and purely.

The benefits of cooking at home are many: it enhances family bonding, saves money, and keeps your family healthier than eating restaurant meals. These are all great reasons for deciding to prepare home-cooked meals. Make your own list for the reasons why you would want to cook at home and let that be your motivator. As many families can attest, even though eating at home is cheaper than eating out regularly, grocery food is the second biggest expense in the budget after the mortgage payments – so, invest wisely.

Laundry

The best way to tackle laundry is to set aside a day or two for getting it done. I set aside one day of the week to do the laundry, which includes getting it washed, dried, folded, ironed, or taken to the dry cleaners. Pick your day and stick to it. If you have a large family, you can pick extra days in the week to take care of the laundry. Make sure your children know which days are for getting the laundry done so that if they will be needing a particular shirt or pants to wear for a special event, they'll make sure those items get washed on a laundry day that falls well in advance of their special occasion (if those items are dirty).

By not doing small loads of laundry every day you will also save on water and energy bills.

Housecleaning

Have you every watched the show *How Clean Is Your House*? If you haven't, I highly recommend it.

This show will surely motivate anyone to get his or her house clean. One thing this show portrays very effectively is the extent to which bacteria and diseases can build up in an unclean home. The purpose of cleaning your home is not just so that it looks pretty and neat, but rather, housecleaning also keeps your home safe for your family by eliminating germs and bacteria.

Because many people hate cleaning, let me just go through some important reasons for why housecleaning is important:

- Having a home is a gift from God – take care of it.
- Having a home is the American dream – take care of it
- Your home is a reflection of you
- Your home is where you live
- Your home is where you will most likely live for many years
- Your home is where you will get refreshed
- Your home is where you will rest

My home is my pride and joy, and housework is a priority item in my life and in my planning. I set aside one day each week for doing all my housecleaning. This day is only for housecleaning – not laundry or running errands – those are done on other days to prevent overload. If you have a cleaning service or a housemaid, no problem, organize cleaning on that day.

The important point here is to make sure you schedule housecleaning into your weekly plan. Housecleaning should not be exempt from your schedule. When you schedule housecleaning, make sure the laundry has been done, perhaps the day before, so you are not worrying about that on the day set aside just for cleaning. You can pick whatever day you like, but my recommendation is to do your housecleaning before the weekend so you have your weekend free to spend with your family and friends.

Car maintenance, including putting gas in the car

Oil changes, car cleaning, and repairs need to be taken care of on a regular basis to extend the life of your car and thus make the most of the investment you spent in purchasing your car. Make a plan and pick a day in the month or week when you will take care of all your car-related duties. Do not neglect to take car of your car. Pay attention to its needs so your car can last and last. Keep it clean, keep oil changes up to date, and keep your tank filled in case of an emergency or gas shortage. Your car deserves attention and care because it takes you wherever you need to go. Doing regular maintenance on your car will either prevent or forestall future mechanical problems your car might have.

Estate planning – saving and planning

Schedule a day for tackling your estate planning. This is normally done about once a year, such as at the beginning of the year, but you can do it as often as you like. In brief, estate planning involves saving, spending, budgeting, planning, developing wills, insurance, and life insurance. Are you saving, planning, and looking after your estate? If you have never done any estate planning, we will delve into this topic later in the book.

House maintenance, lawn care, and repairs

If you own or rent a home, taking care of it is another facet of daily life. The outside of the house needs to be maintained and cared for just like the inside of the house. The lawn needs to be mowed, weeds need to be killed, and the garden needs to be cared for. Planning a specific time to take care of these tasks ensures that they are done in a timely manner and routinely, which keeps your home looking beautiful. Schedule time to get these things done, and if you own your home, see to it that it is maintained in tiptop shape. You will be happy and so will your home. Your neighbors will be thrilled too! Scheduling house maintenance alleviates the stress of having to run around taking care of things at the last moment. There is no need for this when good, sound planning keeps things running smoothly. If you keep your home well maintained, then whenever you are having a party or any type of gathering at your home, then the most you will need to do is a few touch-ups because you will have already been doing a good job keeping it up to date. Nice, huh?

Personal growth planning, including kids

This is also an important aspect of life that you need to manage on a daily basis. Are you reading books? Are you attending any seminars? Are you figuring out what areas you would like to grow in? Are you constantly stretching yourself to learn more and have more of an impact in this world? Do you consistently attend church? Do you attend a small group or Bible study? We will dive into the topic of personal growth later on.

Entertainment planning

Everyone needs some entertainment. Not every day should be taken up with work and planning. Set aside some time for recreation and entertainment, such as a movie, or dinner out, date night or whatever you like. Rock climbing anyone? Plan events that are fun for you and your family. Make it a habit to build recreation and entertainment into your schedule so that your family can get a break from work or school on a regular basis.

Vacation planning

Everyone should have a vacation at least once a year. With good planning and a schedule – I will share some examples with you a little later on how to do that – every family can enjoy some time off. Want to go to Paris? Plan for it and you will see that it is possible. Effective planning will help you capture the possibility of going anywhere you like. Along with saving for your vacation you need to include determining the budget, the time, where will you be staying, making reservations, purchasing plane tickets if you have to fly to the location where you choose to go, and what you want to accomplish when you're there. If you get the basics planned, you don't have to worry what you will do day to day. You'll have the peace of mind to let your vacation unfold in a relaxing manner.

Mentoring and coaching planning

Are your privileged to be able to mentor someone or coach someone? If so, then God bless you! Are you scheduling regular monthly meetings and time with them? If not, take heart and begin to plan time to mentor the ones God has placed in your life who look to you for guidance.

Unexpected events planning

I know it is kind of hard to predict or know when unplanned events will come along, but if you keep in mind that unforeseen events can happen at any time, you won't be discouraged when they come along. You'll find that you're more able to calmly work around your scheduled plans to adapt to those unforeseen events.

Everything we do determines whether we spend money, save money, give money away, or waste money. Many people waste money carelessly, and then they wonder what happened. They ask themselves, *How did I get here?* On the contrary, good money management eliminates these needless questions because it addresses how you can bring financial purity to your portfolio.

Lazy days

We all have lazy days and for that matter, we all *need* lazy days. Be sure to plan a day to do nothing but relax, preferably on the Sabbath day after you get home from church. It is okay to do nothing once a week, as commanded by God. Some people feel like they constantly need to be doing something and cannot rest. Then they break out in cold sores, get sick in other ways, and they wonder why. Part of it is from not getting enough sleep, but it is also from not giving your body the rest it needs. Even God gave Himself a day of rest after creating the heavens and the earth in six days, and He gave us a day off for a reason. Even the strongest of bodies need rest and relaxation. There is no way around it. If you push your body hard enough, eventually it will suffer.

I have found that having a list helps me stay organized and ensures everything gets done in a timely manner, such as getting bills paid on time, making sure the oil in my car gets changed when it needs it, and shopping for a week's worth of dinners so that I'm not caught unprepared and thus have to spend more money eating out. I also make sure my work day is planned accordingly so I can keep all my meetings and appointments on time.

What I did not include on my to-do lists is when I check my emails, and other small things like that. I simply roll that task into my "getting ready" time in the morning and in the evening between commercials when I am watching TV; in other words, I multi-task and check emails when I'm also getting something else done. You can make your to-do list as it applies to the tasks, projects, and important events in your life.

I still have three free days in the week to see my friends and do fun stuff. On Saturday when I do my shopping, it is mainly for food and household items. I do most of my clothes shopping three times a year and online primarily. This saves me a lot of time because I normally browse the catalogs between breaks or time spaces I have available during the day, highlighting what I want, and then I purchase what I've chosen during my scheduled shopping time. I only look at the catalogs about twice a year to keep from tempting myself to buy outside of my timeframe and to keep myself from spending impulsively on things I do not need. I make sure I only receive a few catalogs to not persuade me otherwise. My point is to not allow any temptation or unnecessary distractions that will take away from the important tasks of the day.

It is important to get things done and to make sure they are done in a timely manner. You can either choose to let the distractions be the order of the day or you can choose to have your very important to-do list be the order of the day. Having your to-do list be the order of the day can also help you avoid any unnecessary spending throughout the day.

We need to follow our to-do list or our plan for the day so that we can keep ourselves on track and avoid any crazy spending, which can easily happen. Keep this in mind when you find doing your to-do list boring and unnecessary. Look at it as a money-saving event or a "get-it-done" motivator. Think of it as a way of protecting your future earnings. If you have children, it is vital to keep a to-do list and a calendar filled with all their important events so your children get all the information and attention they need. Visits to the doctor, dentist, sports practices and games, and other events become too much for us to remember, and relying on our memory is not the best method to use. There are plenty of organizers and agendas to help keep us on track so that we remember everything. If you have a computer or a laptop, it is most likely equipped with a calendar program that has pop-up reminders of when you need to do something. It is a great thing to use because it's a visual reminder, and it only takes a few minutes to plug in your events and special tasks you need to complete. Whether you manage your projects on a handwritten calendar or in a binder-type agenda, or through a computer program, doing so can be extremely helpful in achieving goals.

Managing your tasks and projects this way also ensures order and completion, something that should be a primary objective for each of us. You should want to get things done and finalized so that you can get to the next project. Building this simple discipline into your life helps it stay interesting and gives you the satisfaction of accomplishment.

The point here is to stay focused on your financial goals so that you are not spending money on any distractions that may come your way – and come your way they will. Be prepared, plan, and take action to protect yourself against any unnecessary distractions, as they can be costly, but they can also rob us of our time as well.

I recommend you have a life plan, a yearly goal-setting plan, a quarterly plan, a monthly plan, a weekly plan, and a daily plan. I know that sounds like work and maybe perhaps to some of you it sounds like a lot of effort, but actually it is quite simple and quick once you get used to such planning on a regular basis.

While there are many books that do an in-depth study on goal setting, I am merely setting the stage for a first-step process into your financial purity portfolio. It is crucial, important, and necessary. Let me explain why: you need to know what you are going to do in life so that you can manage your money accordingly, meaning, how you will save it, develop it, stretch it, and grow it.

You might be thinking, *Well, I just need to get by day by day. I can't look too far into the future when it comes to my finances.* I am challenging you to change your vision. Be a great thinker and do not see the smallest of smallest things but the biggest of the biggest things. That is how you can turn your life around and make things happen and make your dreams come true. Fight for what you want in life and go for it.

I truly believe having goals in life is almost magical because it gives you a sense of purpose and determination. It also helps to provide motivation for everyday life because you begin to dream, then you try and figure out how to make your dreams come true. If you have dreams you want to fulfill, whether small or big, translate those dreams into goals that are written down on paper. I am an avid supporter of having dreams, and I do not think there are any dreams too big to write down on paper.

Organization and planning are an important step in your financial purity portfolio. Take heart and develop a planning process that works for you and that is appropriate for you and your family. Once you get into the habit of planning your days and projects, it will become second nature to you and you will soon find yourself doing it all the time. Be creative and develop a system that speaks to you and your family.

Chapter 3

Tithing Purely

Of everything you give me, I will faithfully return a tenth part to you. Genesis 28:22

Christ commands us to give. He also expects us to give willingly and wisely. This is an important part of our Christian life and walk.

A big part of your money management portfolio should be giving or tithing as it is called in the Bible. Before reading on, make sure you are willing from your heart to give generously with no hidden agendas. It is completely up to God to determine what your blessings will be. You should not tithe expecting something in return or because someone has helped you. Yes, it is nice to help someone who has helped us, but to help someone because our heart desires to do so is a blessing.

You should tithe because God calls us to. We are to tithe as if God Himself was asking us to do so, because He is. This is what I call tithing purely, and it is an integral aspect of your financial purity portfolio. Tithing purely means to give because God asks you to and for no other reason. Sometimes our pride and human emotions want to take it further and brag, "Look what I did," or we expect God to grant us the winning lottery ticket. That should not be the case. We are to give purely, honestly, and with integrity. Tithing is good and wise. You never know who needs help out there; even if you feel that your income is limited, there is always someone else who is struggling even more, and they can benefit from your generosity. There are so many people out there that need a helping hand that it would be hard *not* to want to give. Do not worry about giving an enormous amount of money; even something small can go a long way.

Sometimes giving doesn't even have to involve money. You can purge your closets and fill up bags of clothing. You can go through your garage and see what you do not need anymore and that is just taking up space and producing clutter. You can go through old items and see what you can give away. Old furniture can help prevent people from sleeping on the floor. Old curtains can help a family whose windows are bare. The next time you clean out your old items, instead of having a garage sale, try giving them to a family in need or a local charity.

Why should we tithe?

We should tithe because God desires us to. Helping others that are less fortunate than us is one of the most selfless acts we can do, and thus it is a privilege. It helps us to think of others, it strengthens our hearts, and God is pleased. There are many people right in our own cities and towns who are hungry and poor. I have a soft spot for them in my heart. Hunger and cold weather are some of the hardest things to bear for a human besides torture. Think about the poor people who have no heat because they cannot afford it. That breaks my heart, especially if there are children in the family.

Tithing builds our relationship with God, and by tithing faithfully we learn to think of others. We gain a strong awareness of what is going on around us and we then get creative as to how we can help. Tithing is good for the soul because it keeps us from becoming greedy.

Where do we tithe and how do we tithe?

Tithe to your church

It is very important to tithe consistently, and a part of your tithes should most certainly go to your church. Your church needs to survive and pay the bills. Help them do that, especially if you are a member. The church leaders need to pay the bills, such as water and electricity, to keep the services going; the telephone bill must be paid so that those in need can contact them when they need to; the building expenses must be met so you can have somewhere to go to church, and the salaries of the pastors and ministers need to be paid so they can minister to you and all the members of the congregation. They need to survive and pay their bills just like you and I have to do.

Many people have told me that they are uncomfortable with tithing to churches due to all the issues of poor money management and embezzlement problems that have plagued so many churches. Here is a word of wisdom for you on that topic: if you are uncomfortable with one church you may be comfortable with another. There are many churches out there that are genuinely interested in helping people grow spiritually. There are churches out there that are also very interested in helping people with any unexpected problems they need to resolve. They will not be able to do that if they cannot survive. You need to find a church that's just right for you and get plugged in. Don't force the issue; take your time and find that one special church for you and your family. Church attendance and involvement is an important aspect of our lives, and there are many churches that manage the money they receive with integrity and wisdom.

Many people have shared with me that they feel the church staff seems to be doing "extremely well" financially and it makes them uncomfortable because they are struggling. They see church staff in homes that are valued at over half a million, or they drive expensive cars and therefore, people cannot help but wonder, *what is the church doing with all the tithes they receive? Are all the tithes going to pay salaries?*

Well, let me share some of my thoughts with you. It is entirely up to God how He determines to bless someone. You cannot interfere with that. There are many cases where the church staff has learned to master the art of investments and they have done a good job of growing their money. They also could have had money in an account from years ago that they have not touched until now. There could be other reasons, like they might have received an inheritance.

You would also be surprised at how frugal and prudent many church staff members can be when it comes to managing their money. Many churches are now focusing on financial classes for their members, and it is doing a world of good.

Until you know the truth and have all the information, don't be quick to assume they are making large amounts of money from the tithes and offerings they receive. Have there been cases where this has happened? Yes. Does it mean it is going on in your church? Not necessarily. If you feel this may be going on, you can always talk to your church leaders and ask to see the church's financial statements. Financials should be readily available for any of the members to review.

There are many churches that support different people and different organizations in the community. Keep in mind that the church leaders need to be concerned about longevity and survivability. The saddest thing to me is seeing a church close their doors. When you hear of a church saving and investing, it is for the purpose of surviving. There is nothing wrong with that; in fact, it should give you a sense of peace knowing that you will have a church home that will be there for some time to come. Nothing complicated, just plain saving and investing. If you have children, think of them and how they will have a church to go to now and in the future, and most of all, they (and you) will have a church you are all comfortable with.

As I said earlier, church is important, and when we have our spiritual lives in order everything around us seems to make sense and we can handle issues that come up with greater strength and ease. Church can be wonderful for keeping us in check and preventing us from drifting away from the Lord. Being involved in church activities is also a wonderful way to build relationships, but none of this can happen unless the church survives, so continue to be faithful in your tithes and remember your church.

Choose a charity to support

When you have a charity or a cause you are passionate about and sensitive to, you will find a way to tithe to them. Not sure of a good charity? What are you passionate about? Feeding the homeless? Visiting orphanages? Helping single mothers? Helping people rebuild their lives? Determine what you are passionate about in your heart and then find an organization that has this similar passion. Then you'll know where you want to give your support.

Remember, there will always be people who need your help, and organizations do their best to stay alive and continue to provide help to those who need it. But again, just like how it is when you tithe to your church, with your generous support and love these charitable organizations can continue on fulfilling the mission they are equally passionate about.

Expectations

Tithing is something that God asks us to do as part of our money management. Tithing should be a big part of your financial purity portfolio. Sometimes as we tithe we start to expect the grandest of things from God like huge mansions and expensive jewelry, for example. As I mentioned to you earlier, it is completely up to God to bless you as He so desires.

It is hard to not want something in return, but when you tithe with humility, you do not expect anything in return. It is normal to feel like you want something in return because we are all human, and sometimes our emotions and feelings can get the best of us, but you need to remember the bigger picture – obedience to God.

Having humility is one sure way to tithe purely, without expecting anything in return. Another way to look at is letting God bless you as He sees appropriate rather than you wanting to be blessed in a certain way or with a certain reward. Tithing purely prevents you from building a hidden agenda in your heart. You may think that no one is watching, but God sees everything. Let Him see you tithing purely without expecting anything in return.

Fears

Many people feel afraid to tithe because they do not have money in abundance and thus they feel threatened to part with it. They feel threatened in the sense that they are giving away whatever little money they have.

The comment I hear over and over again is, "When I hit the lottery, then I will tithe," or, "When I get rich, then I will give money away." If you are following God's commands and trusting in Him, there is no need to have any fears. Tithing is not about giving money because you have a lot of it but because you are obedient to God and because you love Him. We are required to tithe ten percent of our income; it doesn't matter how much money you make. Do not go by what everyone else is giving. You give according to what you can give and how you feel led by God. Refrain from comparing.

If you feel you cannot commit to tithing ten percent at first, then start small until you reach the ten percent that God asks us to give in His Word. If you cannot give in a small way then it will be hard to give big. With discipline, obedience, prayer, and the desire to help others, you can overcome any fears you may have.

Again, if you're struggling with the fear that your church is mismanaging the money they receive in tithes, find a church you are comfortable with, as there are many churches out there that have a true interest in helping the community. Ask the church staff how they are involved in the community, and visit the churches several times until you feel that all your questions are answered. Most importantly, do you feel that you are spiritually growing through the messages and small groups your church offers? This is also another factor for you to consider when looking for a church you are comfortable with being on the receiving end of your time, talents, and tithes.

Pressure

Can we feel pressured to give to a cause or to an organization? Yes, it is possible, very much so. If you feel pressured by an organization or a charity to make a donation and you feel uncomfortable doing so or are simply not sure, then step back and pray about it. It may not be a wise decision for you to give to that particular organization or charity at that time. Remember, tithing should be done joyfully from your heart and should be something you have prayed over with God. If you feel pressured and obligated to give to a certain organization, then check your concerns. Why do you feel pressured or feel obligated to give to this particular organization? Maybe God is asking you to give somewhere else. Pray about it until your concerns are lifted and you feel comfortable enough to make a decision.

Tithe and Give Quietly

If someone such as a friend or a family member has asked you to help them because they are going through a rough patch, do so with discretion. If you are willing and able to help someone financially, know that it was probably very challenging for them to ask you for help to begin with. Refrain from telling other people about the situation so that you can protect the family you are helping. There is no need for you to share this with anyone else, not even as a "prayer request," as it is a private matter between the two of you. Even if the person who asked you for help has not asked you to keep the matter private, it is wise to not share their situation with others. If they choose to share their experience with someone, then let that be their choice. You as the helper need to be sensitive and wise about other people's feelings. Your position should be one of delight, discretion, confidence, wisdom, good-heartedness, and genuine concern. Refrain from gossiping to friends and other family friends, as this can be very hurtful and humiliating. Difficult times can happen to all of us, and we never know when it will be "our turn" to need help.

Keep your tithes to yourself. What you tithe you do not need to broadcast. Keeping your tithes, gifts, and donations quiet is a wise choice. There is no need to have everyone know about it. If you believe in a cause, then standing up for what you believe in is honorable. The work and the time you put in is also honorable and is often public. Sometimes this level of involvement is public because you have to speak up and out about what you believe in. However, what you donate, give, or tithe should remain behind closed doors. There is no reason to shout this to the world, for if you are not careful, your motives can become clouded. It is easy for us to get "pride creep." We want to tell everyone what we've given because it puffs up our pride and makes us feel better.

Tithing is not always in the form of money; it can be in the form of time and effort. Giving of your time and effort can greatly help those in need. Are you knowledgeable in a certain area and someone needs your help? Give it. Does someone need guidance before making a big decision and they need your input? Give it. Are you talented in a particular area and you can offer it to someone who can benefit? Give it.

Be creative; be aware of the ones whom *you* can uniquely help, and pray about your tithing. Ask God to guard your heart to prevent "pride creep" from coming into your heart.

Bragging

Tithing is not something to brag about, and should be between you God. You give what you know that God is calling you to give. What does God call us to give? Ten percent. This is the only time God dares us to test Him – there is no other reference in the entire Bible where God tell us to test Him and see what He can do. Consider that to be a great motivator to help you cast out all your fears.

Bragging that you tithed this much or that much does no one any good. It can make the organization or the person you helped feel really bad and uncomfortable, and sometimes your motives can be questioned as a result. You do not want to be the cause of that or to be put in that position. Tithe with humility and gratefulness – yes, in gratefulness. God has done so much for us; He is extremely generous with us, and sometimes we do not even realize or understand this. There are many ways to tithe with purity, and bragging is NOT one of them. So if you have bragged, keep that in the past and move forward with humility. Ask God to help you maintain humility in your heart as you tithe, and specifically ask Him to help prevent you from getting "pride creep." When the urge comes over you to brag, or you justify your thoughts by telling yourself that you simply have the desire to "share" with others what you've given, ask God to guide you and guard you.

Just how much should we share with other people about our tithing activities? Well, if you are asked, you can share that you do tithe and leave it at that. Letting people know that you are obedient and that you tithe can teach someone a thing or two about your heart. Where you tithe can also be something safe to share. If you are asked for more details from someone outside of your family, you can say that you tithed what you felt God asked you to do, and this way you let the person know that you are not comfortable with sharing anything further. Now, keep in mind there may be someone who is really curious to know what you do so that they may follow in your footsteps, or maybe they're a young Christian who needs guidance. You can always guide them to follow the instructions in the Bible or give them a book (such as this one!) that teaches biblical truths about our financial responsibilities. You need to distinguish the motive and the need of the person so you can determine the best way to help them and protect yourself. Do not feel obligated to share your tithes if you do not want to, even if you are asked.

Believe it or not, bragging, sharing, and telling everyone or some people what you gave to this organization or that cause is very common, and people feel a need to do it in order to be heard and to convince those around them that they are caring people. Check your heart and tithe with humility.

Some ideas...

Something I have done in my financial purity portfolio is open up several checking accounts for easier management of different aspects of my spending. I have opened up a separate checking account just for tithing. The account has its own checks and its own debit card with a separate design on the card as a visual reminder to me. Banks now offer all kinds of different designs you can choose from, and having different designs on your checks and debit cards helps you to be organized. All tithes, giving, support, and activity on this particular checking account is monitored separately. I do not blend the money with what I have in my regular checking accounts, because this may cause confusion.

All tithes that I plan to give are then deposited into this account, and this account is utilized exclusively for tithing and giving. There is no buying anything on the account. It is only used for tithing. Using this method also helps you have a good visual of where your money is going, and you do not need to worry about any confusion if something else was purchased by mistake. It is a great system that works well for me. You may have a system that works for you and that is great. Whatever organization system works for you, implement it and use it faithfully.

Let's recap...

- Tithing is important to your spiritual walk with God
- Tithe to your church
- Tithe to a charity you are passionate about
- Tithe gleefully, never with expectations

- Avoid bragging
- Avoid “sharing” with others what you have tithed
- Tithe with humility and gratefulness
- Guard against “pride creep”
- Pray about your tithing

Chapter 4

Prayer

Rejoice always, never cease praying, render constant thanks; such is God's will for you in Christ Jesus. 1 Thessalonians 5:16-18

You may be wondering, *Why is the topic of prayer in a book about money?* The answer is simple: we should be praying over our finances just like we pray over any other area of our life. Prayer is so important that we should not neglect it in any area of our life. We should be diligently praying every day concerning every aspect of our life. We build our relationship with God through prayer because it allows us to communicate with Him. Daily prayer strengthens us and gives us the grace and courage to face each and every day.

The financial market has given everyone their fair dose of worries, anxieties, concerns, and fear. Why are we worrying so much? Why are we almost in panic mode? I know people who do not have any investments or even a 401K, thus they have lost no money, and they are panicked about the market! One day I asked someone what they were so worried about, and they replied that the "market is bad." I then asked them how that affected them since they didn't invest in the stock market, they still had there job with a company that was doing well, and they didn't have an answer. It is one thing to be concerned about the market, and yes, I am concerned, but I am not in panic mode. I still enjoy life.

If you are going to be worried, make sure you know why you are worried. Don't be worried just because other people are worried; it is not healthy for you, and needless worry takes your focus off the things that matter to you. Prayer keeps us grounded in the security of the Lord, not in the things of the world.

Sometimes we don't think it is important to pray. We think that God doesn't see the importance of praying about our finances, and therefore we don't pray. I have had many people tell me that there are more important things to pray about than their money. God cares about everything in our lives, not just some things as some may think. Another reason we may not pray is because we do not have time or we say we will do it later.

Why don't we pray?

- Laziness
- Procrastination
- Lack of time – or at least that's what we think
- We don't see the importance of prayer

Many people don't pray because they are lazy. It is that simple, but laziness goes a long way to take us nowhere. Many times we say that we will do it later, and then when later comes we continue to say that we will pray later and then later again. Before you know it you are caught up in a vicious cycle of telling yourself, "I will get it done later." Prayer should not be seen as a chore but as a privilege available to you.

I know that most of us have our days jam-packed with a loaded to-do list, but we should still make time for God through prayer and time spent alone with Him. Even if you start out with a couple of minutes, something is better than nothing. Once you are in a routine of prayer, praying will become a priority and you will have time in your day for prayer.

Many people do not see the importance of prayer, so therefore they do not pray. Sometimes I wonder if we truly understand that when we pray we are speaking directly to the Lord. I think if we knew exactly what happens when we pray we would be careful to not miss a day of prayer.

Why *should* we pray?

- To keep our relationship strong with God
- To squash all our fears about the financial market
- To give us strength daily
- To gain wisdom
- To give us peace
- So we can rely on God and not on the world.

Prayer is crucial to our daily walk with God. We need it, and deep in our spirits we want it because we feel good when we pray. Prayer, however, is not your ticket to get what you want (or what you think you want). The primary reason for prayer is communication and closeness with our Lord.

Prayer gives us the courage to face life every day and not give in under any circumstances. When we pray, we strengthen ourselves to face everyday life with grace and purity. Through prayer we gain the strength and wisdom we need to help others and offer them encouragement, wisdom, and inspiration.

Through the grace that regular prayer brings into our lives we can tolerate things easier and interact with others more patiently. When problems arise we tend to be gripped with fear and worry, and we are not at peace. We cannot control what goes on in the financial market, but we *can* control how we handle ourselves. Through consistent prayer and a quiet time with the Lord, our strength is built so that we can handle everyday life with stability, level emotions, wisdom, and peace.

What should we pray for?

- Everything

- Wisdom in building a good credit score
- Wisdom in building a good credit report
- Wisdom to get out of debt (if you have debt)
- Wisdom in making big financial decisions, such as purchasing a home
- Direction concerning how to achieve your financial goals

We really need to be praying over everything – and our family, work, and finances are no exception. We need to bring everything before God and share our concerns, worries, and celebrations with Him. Prayer should not just be for the bad times, but for celebrating the good things with the Lord as well.

Pray for wisdom in building a good credit score and a good credit report. To accomplish this, are you studying your purchasing habits? Are you aware of what is influencing your credit score? Pray for wisdom so you can act accordingly in your financial affairs.

Do you have debt you are trying to pay off? Are you prayerfully working on a plan to get out of debt and pay everything off? Are you staying away from purchasing anything major so you can focus on your debt? Are you praying for the willpower to be diligent and consistent in paying off your debt? Are you looking for opportunities to earn additional income so you can pay down your debt?

Pray for wisdom in making good choices when it comes to your money. Do you need to buy that car? Can you save for the car instead? Can you wait a year or two? Do you have to make that purchase decision now? Do you need to take out that loan? There are many things we need to be praying about. Pray over everything you do when it comes to your money. Don't assume you do not need to pray for your finances, because you do. Your finances are important to God.

Pray over the direction you want your finances to take. Ask God to guide you and teach you wisdom when it comes to your finances. Keeping your finances stable requires effort, and part of that effort is prayer. Don't neglect prayer in such an important area of your life. What is happening now, tomorrow, and in the future is very important, and you should be seeking guidance, praying, and studying the Word of God for guidance.

How should we pray for our finances?

There is no right or wrong way to pray, but effective prayer must come from a heart of humility and gratitude. We should never pray just to "get things" or to win the lottery. That is not the purpose of prayer; it is not a goody pill we can take to make everything be just the way we want it.

It always surprises me to hear how many people turn bitter when they pray to hit the lottery and then don't. I know one person who is an atheist because of people who have prayed such things and have not had their prayers answered. This was their "ticket" and their "confirmation" that there is no God. This saddens my heart greatly. We cannot command God to give us what we want, especially if what we are asking for is not good for us.

You may think that falling into debt is a bad thing. I would like to suggest, however, that you take your experience and turn it into a good one. Falling into debt and then paying off your debt can be a fantastic thing to experience. Let me show you:

- You develop experience when it comes to money
- You learn to be frugal
- You learn to be patient
- You practice great money management skills
- You can use your experience to teach others

I think this is a wonderful experience. Granted, going through the experience may be challenging and you may feel defeated at times, but take heart! When you come out at the other end of the tunnel you are sharper, wiser, and more cautious about how you spend your money. You are more diligent about saving and spending. Most importantly, you are then able to teach others. I think that is fantastic!

You can very well be great at money management even though you have not had any debt in your lifetime. All I am saying is that any experience, even a seemingly bad one, can be a good learning tool.

Your financial purity portfolio should contain the important component of prayer. Develop a habit of praying over your finances, read the Bible, and make wise financial decisions. Once this becomes a regular part of your life, you might just find yourself asking, *Why would I **not** pray about my finances?*

Chapter 5

Vices That Steal Our Money

Dearly beloved, I beseech you as strangers and pilgrims, abstain from fleshly lusts, which war against the soul. 1 Peter 2:11

What is a vice? The simplest answer is that it's an aspect of our character that is a moral weakness. Vices are also commonly referred to as bad habits. While there are many vices, this chapter will focus on the primary vices that can or in many cases literally *do* rob us of our money. We find it hard to admit that these things rob us of our money because we are voluntarily paying for them. Many times we do not see the effects vices can have on our finances over the short-term and the long-term, for that matter. Yes, there are vices we partake of that cost us money.

We tend to see vices as being merely forms of enjoyment or sources of pleasure. Some we know are dangerous and others we tend to justify as being normal and completely okay to partake in. It is very easy for us to defend that which we like, and we see nothing wrong with it. Then we find that little by little we get more and more involved in these vices. Little by little we spend more and more money on these vices. What can be ten dollars today turns into hundreds of dollars tomorrow. Little by little our soul gets addicted to such vices and we drift apart from God, leaving our walk with Him a faded memory. Ask anybody that is addicted to drinking or drugs and they will tell you they never "intended" to become addicted when they first "tried" it (usually there is no "trying" – there's just the first time of many more to come). We can never underestimate how strong or how weak our body can be. Some people can withstand a first try and walk away from an addictive substance without thinking twice. Others cannot. You never know which one you will be.

We will take a look at these vices, what they do, and what they can cost us, not only to our finances but also to our spirit, which is priceless. Sometimes we think that a few fun moments can be cheap or "harmless." I exhort you to consider how unsafe these vices can be and how costly they can be to you spiritually, emotionally, physically, and financially.

While there are different kinds of vices that can easily rob of us of our money, this list includes the vices that the majority of people spend their money on.

What are the vices I am referring to?

- Smoking
- Gambling
- Drinking / Alcohol
- Strip bars
- Psychic hotlines
- Psychics
- Witchcraft
- Mediums
- Palm reading
- Tarot cards
- Crystal ball readings
- Sex outside of marriage
- Porn subscriptions
- Drugs

Let's take a look at these vices, which seem to get the best of our money, and in some cases, our body and spirit as well.

Smoking

Some say that a smoker who has smoked his or her whole life has spent what could have been a small fortune in a 401K account. Smoking is not free, and those who smoke spend. Not only do they fund the habit itself, but they also have to fund everything else that comes with it: buying ashtrays, paying more to have clothes dry-cleaned to remove the smell, having to pay a higher life insurance premium, spending more in healthcare because smokers tend to get sick more frequently than non-smokers do, and the list goes on.

Smoking is very expensive no matter how you look at it. The cost of a pack of cigarettes averages between $3.50 and $5.95 depending on the state you live in. The average cost per carton of cigarettes is between $5.07 and $22.04 depending on the state you live in. These average prices do not reflect any specific brand. Some smokers are puffing all throughout the day, and some smokers even pride themselves on being very talented with the shapes they can make as they puff out the smoke. Either way, a smoker is a smoker, and most smokers buy at least a pack of cigarettes.

Let's consider the cost of smoking. The average smoker smokes about 10-13 cigarettes a day, which is half a pack. That can cost anywhere from $10.50–$17.85 a week or $42–$72 a month. In many cases this amount of money could be used to pay a bill or could be put into a savings account. Naturally these costs increase the more cigarettes someone smokes.

But because a smoker is fueling a habit they enjoy or that is hard to break, they continue to do it without realizing what a heavy drain it is on their monthly budget. It becomes such a big expense that other more important expenditures are compromised in order to fuel the habit.

If you're a smoker, please keep this in mind: the tobacco companies are getting richer, and you are not. Smoking not only makes you sick, but you end up smelling like a chimney, you age faster, your teeth turns yellow, and in some cases they turn brown, and then you have to spend money to get them whitened. Not only are you funding a vice that has become a habit and a health risk, but you are spending money cleaning up the after-effects as well.

Since we know that smoking can lead to serious health risks, your medical expenses are most likely greater than those of a non-smoker. Here are a few health risks smoking can cause you; every single one of these will force you to spend even more of your money that you could otherwise be saving in your bank account to use for something much better, such as a nice vacation:

- Increased frequency of colds, chest colds, and bronchitis
- Asthma
- Headaches
- Insomnia
- Heart murmur
- Smokers' hack
- Wrinkles
- Pre-mature aging

- Shortness of breath
- Arthritis
- Cancer of the lip, tongue, pharynx, larynx, and bladder
- High blood pressure
- Influenza
- Impaired hearing
- Mental depression
- Stained teeth, fingers, and hair
- Others

A couple of years ago I met the parents of some of my friends, and I was stunned at how quickly they had aged for being only fifty years old. They looked like they were eighty, and that is being generous. They had deep and extensive wrinkles all over their body and looked heavily aged. Surprisingly, they were quick to admit they were smokers or at least had been. It was then that I realized for the first time the effects smoking can have on aging, which is especially evident in the skin.

Why do I mention this? Because more often than not, people end up having plastic surgery to remove the effects smoking has had on their skin. This is an additional expense and one that probably not be necessary if they hadn't smoked in the first place.

Again, smoking is not cheap. If you rent a car and smoke in the car, they will charge you approximately $125 depending on the car rental company and the state you are located in. That is because the smell of smoke is hard to remove. Many noses can detect the slightest hint of smoke and people who end up renting the car after you complain and request a new car.

If you are a smoker and wish to sell your car one day, it will be difficult to sell because not many people want to buy a smoker's car. Your best bet would be to disclose right from the get-go that you smoked in the car, because if a non-smoker is considering buying it, they will detect traces of the smell immediately, even if you have cleaned it.

The bottom line is that smoking costs you a small fortune over the course of your lifetime. If the health risks of smoking do not motivate you to quit, perhaps the cost of smoking will help you quit. If you remain a non-smoker, you'll be amazed at how much more money you suddenly seem to have.

Gambling

What can sometimes be just having fun to one person can be a disastrous addiction for someone else. It may seem harmless to some, but before you know it you are going gambling every week or every chance you can get. You start gambling with just $20 then $40 then $60...all because you won something at first and so you want to keep on trying to see if you can win something else.

You get excited, then you get motivated, then you get determined, then you get hooked, and then you are addicted. Welcome to the vice many people are addicted to: Gambling. Casinos and online gambling games make a tremendous fortune every year.

Gambling is not something God endorses, supports, or blesses. It will leave you broke, and some people end up having to go to therapy to get over their gambling addiction, which costs them even more money. Some people can walk away after having lost $20, but there are plenty others who cannot. The sad thing is that many people do not know they could or would ever get addicted to gambling until they are deep into it. So how can we make sure we never get caught in this vicious cycle? Read scripture and pray to guard your lifestyle. If you feel you are addicted to gambling, or you are spending too much money at the casinos, then pray for strength to resist.

Take a look at the spending habits of a gambler and you will see that they are not honoring God, nor are they keeping their finances in pure order. Are you using a small amount of your hard-earned money to go gambling with when you could have put the money toward paying off credit card debt or toward paying one of your regular monthly bills?

Gamblers always think they will win money every time they go to the casino, and then if they don't win, they think that if they try again with another $10 then will win more and more, which they think will be enough to make up for the money they've spent to reach that elusive goal. Not so. Most people end up spending more money than winning any money. That's what keeps casinos in business. If you like to gamble and have a habit of gambling, take a good look at how much money you are spending. Take a good look at your motivation behind your love for gambling. Keep track of what you spend by writing it down every time you spend. Then take inventory of how much money you are earning. This will serve as an eye opener to where your money is going and if you are incurring a profit or a loss.

I know someone who tries to spend money at every gambling location that comes his way. He loses every time, but he tells everyone he breaks even and does not lose any money. That is another thing gambling can produce in you – denial. You find it difficult to see what is going on because you are having such a good time; you refuse to see what is happening to your finances and to yourself because you don't want to face those difficult truths.

Gambling, for the most part, is not going to make you rich. It will, however, keep you involved until you end up losing money. There is an expression that is said over and over again: "The house always wins!" Win they do, and thus, you lose.

Drinking

Drinking is probably one of the most favorite vices that many people waste their money on. Drinking in moderation can add to our celebrations of cheer and love, especially around the holidays. But most people who drink do so much more frequently than this. Many people, both young and mature, are negatively affected by their drinking habit. Even though some people have not had a bad experience other than passing out on their couch, others have caused car accidents and then later do not remember what happened. This is what the vice of alcohol can do to you.

Now let's take a look at the cost of this vice in terms of money. There are drinkers who spend a good chunk of their money on a consistent supply of booze. An average drinker can spend up to $1,000 a month on keeping up with their drinking habits. Besides the fact that drinking gets the best of you, wipes out your memory, and gets you to do stupid things, people keep on drinking. The drinkers keep on being drinkers.

Drinking can be quite costly, especially when the habit is maintained over the course of many years. Drinking not only hurts your financial purity portfolio (because I seriously doubt God endorses the use of your money for drinking, but God gives you that choice to make), it also affects your physical and mental health. While some people may enjoy an occasional social drink, many people drink more often than not for no particular reason. This is where we can honestly say that drinking dips into our financial purity.

Let's take a look at the cost of drinking at a single sitting. At the time of writing this book I joined some young people at an event to observe their drinking habits. One of them was drinking beer and had ten beers that night. Each beer cost $4.95 + tip so he gave $6 for every beer. He drank 10 so he spent $60. I do not know about you, but that is a big chunk of change. According to this individual, he would drink like this every week or every other week. If it is every week, then that translates into $240 a month, which is $2,880 a year! Just on beer!

On another note, he is always broke. That is because he makes very little money and he spends most of it pretty quickly. If this describes you as well, it is my sincere hope that when you see how much you could be saving rather then spending, it will serve as a great motivator to keep your finances in order. If you've set a goal to improve your financial purity, you can see how it makes sense both financially and spiritually to give up such wasteful spending on drinking.

Every time you drink you lose brain cells that you will never regain. Many people do not know that some drinks are made up of uppers and downers, and the mix can be damaging to the body. If you are not aware of these negative effects then you will most probably drink for the purpose of having a good time, or because you like the taste of the drinks, and then you will continue to drink over and over again all night long and end up spending $30–$40 a night in drinks alone when you could be using that money for something else more important to your life, like paying a bill or buying something that you need for the family.

The people who eventually kick the habit are usually the ones who have gone through rehab. What a shame that so often it has to get to this point; furthermore, this is yet another expense the drinker (or his/her family) must bear. These are the drinkers who have a serious problem with drinking and are in need of help. By the time they end up in rehab they have needed an intervention for a long time because they were chronically addicted to booze. There are even those who have suffered from alcohol poisoning and still continue drinking. They have no control over it. If any of this describes you, please remember that not only is it getting the best of your wallet, but it also makes you sick. Sometimes you get so drunk that you cannot even remember what you were doing. I do not know about you, but anything that causes me to not remember what I've done or where I've been just scares the daylights out of me.

I value my memory and my thoughts. To have that completely removed from me is not something I am willing to deal with. Remember, there is always a reason why God says that you shouldn't do something or why He commands you to stay away from something. Remember, alcohol and the habits of drinking can rob you of your money. Many times a heavy drinking habit can wipe your entire paycheck clean and leave you with nothing to pay the bills. Is this what you want? Do you really want to remain poor because of something you are addicted to? Don't let yourself fall into this trap; protect your money and keep your finances pure.

Let's take a look at some reasons why people drink:

1) They try to anesthetize their problems

People drink because they like the buzz they get, which helps them forget their day and feel good. Drinking seems to be the perfect way for them to erase their problems. Yes, people like this way better than seeking God for help. They do not want to go to their Bible and read the Word to help them deal with their problems. Yes, the answers are in the Bible; it is God's Word for all time, and it can help us.

2) People want to forget their day

People drink to just relax and forget the troubles of their day. Because booze tastes delicious to the drinker, you want to drink more and more of it. You get the buzz and you want to keep the buzz, so you keep drinking and drinking to make sure you are keeping the buzz, but what is happening in the meantime is that you're getting drunk, but you do not realize it because you are about to pass out. Many times, people cannot recognize what is going on because they are already drunk. What started out to be "just something to make you feel good" has now made you sick. My fellow readers, what can make you feel good and stay feeling good is reading the Bible and praying.

3) People just like to drink

Many people think that a good meal should be accompanied with a good glass of wine or some kind of drink. While I think that a nice glass of wine is great with a good meal, especially if you are in good company, you have to exercise control over how many drinks you can consume with the dinner. Many people just keep opening up the bottles of wine, and before you know it your group is on its second or third bottle of wine. The problem with this is that if you plan to drive yourself home and you get stopped by the police and they test you for alcohol, you will get a DUI. All it takes is one glass of wine or a beer to fail the breath test. We all know what happens when you get a DUI. Even though you may not consider yourself to be drunk, the law still considers you to be a hazard on the road, therefore you will get a DUI. Be cautious the next time you want to drink even if it is just one glass of wine. Keep your money in check as well and be sure to spend wisely and stay healthy.

4) People drink to ease tension

People say that drinking helps ease tension. While this may be true up to a certain point, I do not recommend it. It is not the best way to relieve tension, financially or health-wise. There are things you can do to help ease the tension and the pain you may have experienced from the day. You can exercise, take a walk, listen to music, laugh along with your favorite TV comedy, watch a movie, read, or work on a hobby that you know always helps to relax you. We all have worries, projects, and things we have to complete in any given day. Did you have a bad day? Were things just really bad and you are feeling so overwhelmed? A great remedy for this is to read the Bible and to pray. There is power in this.

5) You were invited to a party

It is hard to say no to a drink at a social party. We almost have no control and we want to blend in, so we chug-a-lug a few beers or some kind of drink just to be part of the party. Then the whole drinking cycle starts again and we are exposed to trouble. Even though you are not spending any money because you are at someone else's party, you still need to get home. You still have the risk of driving home if you are not with someone who hasn't been drinking, and you still have the risk of getting stopped by the police and being given a DUI.

Remember, people have died in car accidents as a result of drinking. This has cost countless dollars in court costs and medical expenses. Many people's lives have been destroyed because of drinking. You might say, "How does this equate to financial purity?" Well, when you are not honoring God with your money and are spending it on things of the world, you are bound to expose yourself to a high risk of trouble. This trouble is usually in the form of spending a lot of money dealing with the law, such as having to pay a fine. Today's laws are very strict when it comes to drunk driving. Pray to remain obedient and wise during any party you are invited to.

Strip bars

Many people, both men and women, are lured by the vice of strip bars. Just as in the case with casinos – where "the house" makes money and the gamblers lose money – in strip clubs, the strippers make the money, and the people watching spend the money.

First let me state unequivocally that you should not even be present at one of these places. All you will see are people who are lost and who do not have God in their lives. Is this something you want to be exposed to? You will end up giving the stripper money every time he or she walks by because you feel pressured to do so. Is this honoring God? Is this keeping your money pure?

Are you demonstrating financial purity when you spend your money on people who are doing things that God forbids? It is not financial purity and will most certainly lead you to violate God's will for your life. Any time you are not utilizing your money in an honorable way or for a godly purpose and instead are using it to fuel an activity that God forbids, you are not achieving financial purity but instead you're incurring financial loss.

Psychic Hotlines

Before I became a born again Christian I was involved with these things. I was sure that they would help me see the things I wanted to know and help me get around any problems I had. I had many fears, and this was one of the ways I would deal with them. I called them, and called them, and then called them some more. I was always in constant anxiety. In addition to that, it racked up my credit card bill, which I had kept in great order for many years, but because the balance was so high from calling psychic hotlines I was not able to pay off the entire bill each month, and I fell into debt.

I had to make small payments little by little which was not something I was accustomed to doing. I had always paid my bill in full every month, which was no more than a couple hundred dollars. But when I began calling psychic hotlines, my bill racked up into the thousands of dollars. It was crazy! I thought I was only calling in for a few minutes and so I was completely unaware of how fast the charges were adding up. The truth was, I didn't realize how often I called. At one point, I think I called every day for about a week. I was sure that it was not going to cost a lot and so I just kept on calling. When I look back on this time period in my life, I realize now that I truly believed the psychics could solve all my problems and take my fears away, when actually the whole experience made me more fearful and in debt.

I was only making $6.50 an hour at the time, and thus I was not holding much money in my savings account either. It was really hard. Because the bill was so expensive, I was not able to pay the bill off in full which is what I liked doing. The monthly minimum amount to pay was pretty high and put a strain on all my other bills too. This was not good. This was the first time I got into debt and was not able to pay it off. I was worried, but little did I know I was not in a good place to be facing this challenge. I had no idea what God said on the subject and the last thing I did was turn to God for help with my problems. It took me years to pay off that bill.

Let's take a look at why people turn to psychics to find a "solution" rather than turn to God.

Worry and fear

We all have problems, but sometimes we get so consumed with worry and fear that we feel we have to turn to someone who seems to have more power than we do, such as these hotlines. We cannot seem to think that God *is* the solution and that He can help us with our problems. We are so consumed with fear that we think only psychics, fortune-tellers, and tarot card readers can deal with our problems. We do not see that God is there and ready to help us with our worries, fears, and financial problems. Sometimes God solves our problems in a way that we wouldn't have thought of, or that we think isn't really a solution at first. Just because it is not our way does not mean that God is not involved or doesn't want to help us, because He does. Sometimes the way God chooses to help us doesn't happen as fast as we would like. That is where we need to exercise prayer and patience. When we pray, we learn to wait on God for the answer.

If we are in debt it does not mean that all the debt will go away quickly; instead, God will use the time it takes us to pay down the debt to build patience in us and to teach us about money management. We will learn about money, our habits, and our visions, and we will learn how to handle debt properly. That may be the best part about how God works with and through us. I believe that when we go through problems, no matter how unpleasant they may be, they serve as experiences that can teach us many lessons.

When I was paying down my debt, it did not go away for about three years. That is how long it took for me to get out of debt. I was determined to pay everything off and not go into bankruptcy. I worked two jobs and I worked sixteen hours a day, and God used the two "human angels" who owned this company as they helped me along the way.

At the time I worked for a very small and young company who knew about my situation and offered to give me as much overtime as they could, provided that I was using it to pay my debt off. I used every resource I could and worked overtime on special projects. It helped, and I worked at this pace for close to two years. I worked every day except major holidays. I was determined to reach my goal, and you should be too if you have debt.

When I was working my tail off and seeing my early twenties slipping away into the past, I learned and learned. While my peers were enjoying vacations at the beach, I was broke for years, living paycheck to paycheck while remaining determined to pay everything off as quickly as I could.

My two angels would give me books and pay for me to attend classes so I could learn about money management. This was God working. By the third year, they also gave me a raise so that I could work exclusively for them and leave my second job, which was a Godsend. I was burned out, tired, and not seeing much progress in the fulfillment of my vision. I spent the third year paying off some of the bigger debts that I had, like that wretched credit card I used to pay for the psychics as well as other credit cards I had racked up during school. When I paid them off, I canceled everything I had and got all new credit cards as soon as my credit score allowed.

Through all of this I learned to stay away from the psychic hotlines; I learned to manage my money better; and I learned that God wants us to go to Him for our problems and worries. Now I can look back with a sigh of relief and think, *Problems solved, lesson learned. Thank You, Lord.*

Not knowing the power of God can get many people to turn to psychics. We think they have the power to solve all of our problems. The scary thing is that they will ask you to do all sort of spells and ungodly activities we should not be involved in. We get excited thinking that is going to help all of our problems, when in fact, it grieves our spirit and takes us farther away from a deep relationship with God. Many times we carry out the advice the person on the other end of the line gives us, not knowing that it will take us away from God and cause us to dig ourselves deeper into debt, thus damaging our financial purity portfolio even further. Make no mistake, calling these psychic hotlines will put us deeply in debt, or give us a high bill to pay, and they will not solve any of our problems. God is the one we need to look to and seek for help.

Witchcraft / Mediums

> *Do not go to mediums or consult fortune tellers, for you will be defiled by them. I, the Lord, am your God.*
> ***Leviticus 19:31***

We should not be looking for advice or for solutions to our problems from mediums or anyone for that matter who claims to have the power to solve your problems. You need to turn to God for the help you need and want. There is no reason why you should ever have to use a medium or anyone similar. If there is anything that you need then you need to look to the Lord for all your help. Let me tell you a little bit about who you are consulting with when you go to a medium: these people are far from the Lord and actually, the one they serve and who inspires them is the Lord's enemy. Only the Lord can really help us deal with and solve our problems. If you visit a medium, your problems are going to end up being even bigger because these people charge money and a lot of it too. Many people who resort to using mediums for guidance are often not aware of the power that God has, which is greater than anything else.

Only God is the answer. When you have problems and need strength, turn to the One who can give you strength and wisdom to see you through what you are experiencing. Read the Bible for answers and remember to stay grounded in prayer.

Crystal ball reading / Palm reading

The people who engage in crystal ball reading and palm reading do not know God. They may say they do, but they do not. Those who truly know God know that He does not work like this.

When I was in college, I had a professor who was racist. By that I mean that she was *really* racist, and I knew she did not like me. We all knew she was a racist because she would let her remarks slide casually by, and they were not complimentary. I did not do anything to her, but for some reason she did not like me. Well, we were scheduled to do an oral report that weighed heavily on our final grade. Rumor had it that she liked – no, *loved* – palm reading, and that everyone who did palm reading for their oral report would get extra points because that topic was endlessly fascinating to her.

So like the good student I was, and being ignorant of how we should stay away from occult-like practices, palm reading was the topic I based my oral report on. I went to the library and did all the research I could to sound like a pro. I ended up getting a B- on it. I felt so mad at myself for doing a report based on what someone else liked and not what I liked.

However, due to my research, I was able to learn a lot about palm reading. Palm reading is mainly used to predict your future, something that always intrigues us. Well, your future cannot be determined based on your palm, but based on what God has in store for you. Rely on God to help you with your concerns and worries, and stay away from such fakes. Don't spend your hard-earned money on people who pretend to know your future by looking at your palm when only God knows what is in store for you.

Tarot cards are also something you do not want to get involved in or rely on. Do not get caught up in the frenzy of a pair of cards "telling" you what is going to happen in your future. Continue to read your Bible for the answers you desire and stay firm in prayer.

Horoscopes are both free and costly, depending on where you go and what you seek. Do not get yourself in the habit of relying on them because they are a silly waste of your time. They tell you nothing and only serve to diminish your reliance on God.

Sex outside of marriage

There is blessed sexual love in marriage, there is pre-marital sex, and then there is sex that is paid for. I do not recommend or endorse any of them except the first one. Paid sex is costly, very costly, and dangerous to your health. It is a sure way to take your entire paycheck and leave you broke. It may sound funny to discuss something like paid sex, but we all know it is out there and there are those who do pay for it. Remember that everything you do is linked to the state of your financial purity portfolio.

You may think that sex outside of marriage might not cost anything, but it most certainly can. You could end up with an unplanned pregnancy, and I mean this for both men and women. If you are a man, then you will need to pay child support until the child is eighteen. If you are a woman, then you will need to deal with your pregnancy and everything else that comes with it: the doctor visits, the hospital bills, the diapers, milk, clothes, and so on. You get the idea.

It is best to wait until you are in a marriage with God's blessing so you can fully enjoy all the blessings and peace He has to offer you. For more on sexual purity and purity read my book ***"Everlasting Purity".***

Porn subscriptions

The porn industry is a multi-billion dollar organization. There are many people who willingly pay for subscriptions, which costs an average amount of $60-$80 a year depending on where you buy it from and what you end up buying. It does not stop there. For videos or anything you might want to see, you have to pay on the spot, usually between $30 – $40. Before you know it you have spent a nice chunk of money that could have gone toward paying a bill or doing something fun with your family.

People might say that looking at porn is harmless because it is done in the privacy of their own home and no one will know. However, it is not harmless to your spirit by any means, or to your financial purity. You still need to address the problem of what this does to your spirit and mind. You still need to address the fact that you took some of your hard earned money to buy them. It gets you addicted and keeps you far away from God. Still willing to spend your money on this vice? Think again, as little by little it can weigh heavily on your finances.

For example, pornography may seem harmless (and some couples claim it is healthy for their marriages) – but as I will point out, looking at porn has a very dangerous effect on our spiritual, emotional, and financial well-being. We have the free will to use, spend, and invest our money as best we can, but the question remains – does pornography glorify God? No. It never will.

Anything that is destructive to your spiritual health will hinder your relationship with God by causing you to drift far from Him. This is a slow process that is almost invisible to you and perhaps to other people as well. Before you know it, your spiritual walk with God has become a faded memory – just like the porn subscription money you spent to get yourself drifting from God. It may seem like a small amount at the time, but what a horror to know that money spent to feed your temptations was the very thing that stunted your walk with God. We all need God in our lives, whether we like to admit it our not; deep down in our being we long for God to love and protect us. We desire to be holy and set apart from the world. Holiness and living a holy Christian walk takes effort and making deliberate wise decisions time and time again. Read the Bible often and remain strong in prayer; these are your best weapons of defense.

Drugs

Another way to surely spend all your money is to become addicted to drugs. There are two types of drugs: prescription medications such as potent painkillers and hard-core illegal street drugs. Both can cause serious addictions. The cost to maintain such a habit can leave you broke, sick, alone, and devastated. If you are ever tempted to buy "just a little" or "to see what it is all about," remember that just a "little taste" or a "little try" can lead you down a path of addiction. You never know how your body will respond to what you are trying. Many people find the best excuse for why they tried a drug, is often blaming someone else for it. In the end they are blown away by the experience and want more and more. Many drugs are so addictive that even if you plan not to take them again after the first try, your body will crave them and you will feel helpless to resist. This is especially true of crystal meth and crack cocaine. You don't necessarily have to like the experience in order for your body to become addicted. That is why it is so important not to even try something once.

Ecstasy is often used at parties and clubs to heighten the party-like experience or give that "extra edge" to boost your "good time." If you are offered these "little goodies" as some people call them, walk away, please. As I said earlier, you never know how your body will react or respond. They can be easily addictive and cause you to desire the pills all the time. It is expensive to fund an addiction; you will have to buy and buy and spend a small fortune, which can corrupt your financial purity. Any time you spend your money on filth and danger, you are exposing yourself to high risk.

Many people do get addicted and do not recover until they go through therapy. Even after receiving professional and medical help, it is easy for a former addict to fall back into drug use again and again. Remaining sober is a struggle and then they are back in rehab, which costs even more money, money that could've been used for something else. The temptation never really goes away. That's why it is easier on you spiritually, emotionally, and financially to resist that temptation in the first place.

Many drugs are illegal; if you are caught with them you can go to jail or get fined. The cost for most drugs is very high; please consider the value of your money before ever buying an illegal drug in search of a "good time." This is a sure way to spend your money the wrong way and not the right way, which is to pay your bills with it and put it in your bank account where it can gain interest.

Drug use is also a sure way to get you very sick, and then you have to add health expenses to your growing list of where your money is going and why you cannot save anything – all because of drugs.

The physical toll on your body is pretty horrendous. Let's take a look at what can happen to you ...

- You start to lose memory and mental sharpness
- You can have delusions and hallucinations
- You cannot make decisions for yourself
- Slurred speech
- Inability to drive
- Liver contamination that could eventually lead to liver cancer
- Risk of getting cancer in any of your organs
- If you are snorting "crack" you can eventually develop a damaged nose, which can lead to poor breathing.
- Ultimately, in some cases, drug use can lead to death

The list could be much longer than this. People wonder why they are so sick. People even go so far as to say that they quit a long time ago so they think they don't have anything to worry about. You still have the same risks. Your body was contaminated with poison for some time, and some damage was done. What kind of damage varies from person to person, but the risk could still be there. Remember, sometimes the first "try" can be free and something that a friend gives you. But if you end up becoming addicted, your "friend" is not going to fund your habit.

Think about your health and your finances. When I think about my finances and my hard-earned money, it becomes MORE than enough motivation for me to make pure choices and avoid the vices of the world that want to rob me. Do the same for yourself. Your body is your temple, and your money is your reward for the work you do; use it well and enjoy it wholesomely.

Cherish what you have and live for God's best. Keep your body pure and free from drugs so you can live well.

Let's recap:

- One "little try" can lead to an addiction
- Drugs have long-term unseen consequences that can pop up at any time even if you have quit and are sober.
- Drugs are expensive and place a heavy toll on your finances.
- Drugs rip your financial purity portfolio apart.

The chain effects of drugs are health, finances, career, legal dealings, fines, and jail time. Is it worth it? Doesn't look like it to me. Think about what is important to you, your health, and your financial development. Don't let the events of the world take these away from you, and don't let your friends influence you into a little "try" for a moment of "fun."

Protect your money and your health. Use your hard-earned money for godly activities. Watch over your finances and see to it that you are constantly doing something for your financial welfare everyday. The fewer problems you have to deal with in regards to your money, health, and legal affairs, the more unaffected and untouched your financial purity portfolio will be.

There are plenty of vices out there that can rob of us of our money. Let's not spend our hard-earned money on vices that God does not approve of and has given us a direct order to stay away from. Be cautious, wise, and diligent, and every time you spend your money take a good, honest look at what you've just spent it on. Your financial purity portfolio is all about utilizing your money for wholesome and godly activities. Read the Bible and pray over your finances like you would pray over anything else in your life. Do not neglect prayer for your finances. Honor God with your money so that it brings glory to Him.

Chapter 6

Debt and Budgeting

Show me your ways, O LORD, teach me your paths.
Psalm 25:4

Debt and budgeting go hand in hand. With good budgeting you can possibly remain out of debt, but without good budgeting it is easy to fall into debt. Why do people fall into debt? The reasons vary: some fall into debt because they cannot earn enough money to make a living and so they resort to paying bills using credit cards; some manage their money poorly; and some just simply overspend.

Yes, I was once in debt but then I got out of debt, and I learned my lesson along the way. I learned about money management, work ethics, budgeting, and wisdom. I also had to build up my credit again, too. I worked hard at it, spending money only on living expenses. I did not spend money on entertainments nor did I buy anything beyond the necessities until I had reached my goal of being debt-free.

I made sure that every payment was paid on time. I paid off the smaller debts first then worked my way up to the bigger accounts I had. It took a lot of focused work to do this, but it was very rewarding work. I learned the ins and outs of credit scores and how they are affected by everything you do financially. I subscribed to a credit score watch service and watched my credit score every month. It told me why my score went up and why my score went down, month by month. I watched it for years (and still do).

If you are in debt and are working on getting out of debt, I highly recommend you sign up for a credit watch service. It will be very revealing for you because it will show you how your financial decisions directly impact your credit score both positively and negatively. It is not that expensive and is most certainly worth doing. You can monitor everything that goes on with your credit, including every time a company pulls your credit report; also, watching your report on a regular basis is sometimes the only way you'll ever know if there are errors in it that need to be corrected.

Debt

There are many ways people fall into debt. They overspend, misspend, and do not pay their bills. They collect an assortment of different credit cards and have trouble keeping up with all of them. They have car loans, signature loans, and a mortgage loan. The primary source of debt most people have is with credit cards and loans. In speaking to many people concerning how they resolved their debt issues, I discovered the following are the most common ways to tackle the problem:

- Pay everything off with your hard-earned money

This wipes your slate clean and gives you great satisfaction that will grant you peace of mind. It may take time, patience, and diligence to pay off all your debts, but the rewards are far greater than you think. Your credit report reflects the good work you did and future creditors will be willing to grant you a loan, especially a mortgage. Your credit score will increase noticeably. You will build resistance to the temptations of shopping, impulse buying, and splurging. You will know the true purpose of money and the role it plays in your life. You will be careful whenever you need to spend money, and will have learned much from this experience. You will be the master of your money instead of it mastering you.

- Declare bankruptcy

In some cases when there are excessive medical bills to pay, the only plausible solution is to file bankruptcy. Sometimes the effort a family goes through because of the long-term illness or injury of one of their loved ones causes them to incur insurmountable debt. The fight to keep their loved one alive is the primary motivation in their life.

Other times, when people have simply mismanaged their money and spent like crazy, they declare bankruptcy. They either get frazzled over the bills they cannot pay or they do not know what else to do, and so they declare bankruptcy.

Whenever possible, paying everything off is the better way to go; after all, when you spent money you didn't have (by using credit cards), you knew at some point that you would have to pay it off.

- Simply do not pay

Not paying will not make anything go away. If you do not pay then your creditor or lender will simply write-off your loan and then send your account to a collection agency. They will never go away. They will find you and hound you day and night if necessary unless you can come to an agreement on payment terms with them. If one collection agency does not collect any money from you, then another one will call you day and night. They might even show up at your door to get anything from you – even $20. Do you want that? Think about it. You will never have peace, and you will constantly find a way to avoid them, which you'll discover is only for a short period of time before they will find you again and again and again. My advice is to stay clear of this road. Keep your finances pure by paying up. Your creditors lent you money thinking you would pay.

Besides, paying will look good on your credit report. If you do not pay then your accounts on your credit report will be coded as a write-off or a charge-off, which is almost worse than having bankruptcy on your credit file. It will stay on your credit report for seven long years, and during that time will make it nearly impossible for you to get a new credit card or a loan. Have children? Think about them and set an example for them to follow so that they can learn properly from you. You are most likely the one person they observe the most. Don't hide anything from them – share and teach. Show what you are doing and why – and teach.

Once you've ruined your credit, if you ever find yourself in an emergency situation and need financial help, almost no lender will be willing to help you except the loan sharks. Yes, they exist! We will talk more about them later. There are also the places that will give you cash if you give them your car title, assuming you have one (and the only way you can have access to your car title is if you own it free and clear and have no loan on it). You see? This is a vicious cycle that will only come and bite you in the end if you do not take the most sacred and honored road – paying off all your debt with your own hard-earned money. This is God's way – follow it hard and heavy. Trust me; God's way is the best way!

If this sounds like I'm describing your situation, I know that you want to move from a life of debt and living paycheck-to-paycheck to a sound and safe financial platform. It is possible and you can do it. Will it happen overnight? I don't think so, not unless you have someone come along and give you an enormous amount of money, and even then you would have to pay off your bills with the money instead of just spending it all (which has happened to people who have won millions in the lottery). But in most cases this does not happen to the ordinary individual. We have to work at it. We have to change our vision and our lifestyle. We have to make conscious decisions to stop doing what we were doing before.

Many people fall into debt and often keep falling into debt because they feel overwhelmed and are not sure what to do. Other people find a way out of debt. Some take the easy road and some take the more difficult road. I prefer the difficult road, which is actually paying everything off with your money that *you* have earned.

How and why do people end up in debt?

I don't think people wake up one day and decide to get into debt. It is a gradual process of spending and overspending habits. I do understand that some families may experience an emergency or a health crisis, but for the most part in this book we are going to examine the typical spending habits that most people have and how those habits get them into debt.

Store Sales

I never have cared about the crazy sales that seem to go on all the time, like after Thanksgiving. I have had friends who wake up at the crack of dawn just to run to the stores to get the after-Thanksgiving sales. Because people think they are getting a good deal on items, they snap them up and come home with bags and bags of stuff that they probably did not need in the first place. The items usually end up in their closets for months and months to either be used later on or given away to a charity. I have always avoided these sales like the plague. Unless I *really* need something (which most of the time I don't), I never go to them.

I contend that you will spend less money buying what you need when you need it than buying something because it is on sale.

This is a dangerous cycle that can get you into spending the money you've worked so hard to earn. It is always a pleasure to buy nice things, especially when they are on sale, but the problem is that most people never just buy what they need on those shopping trips. They see discount signs and think it is okay to buy items just because they are on sale. Before they realize what has happened they have spent hundreds of dollars in one store, and yet they still think they are saving money because the items were marked down slightly! Yikes! Then what? They go to the next store and then the next, and then when they get home their spouse is in shock at the receipts, and then comes the credit card bill at the end of the month, and on and on the story goes.

Even if you are wealthy and can buy whatever your heart desires, it is still not a good habit to do so. You are only keeping the stores rich. Unless you truly do need the items you end up buying, then **I highly recommend you buy only what you need *when* you need it.** If you end up benefiting from a sale, then fantastic! Otherwise, spend your money and your time on other things that matter. Shopping is not the only thing to do in life, and it really is not your best friend.

Many people find comfort in shopping when they're going through a depressing time in their life, like when they've been left by a boyfriend or girlfriend or their beloved pet has passed away. But the reality is that shopping will not change anything; it will only give you a temporary feeling of self-worth. It will not remove the blues you are feeling. We will all go through times of sadness as well as cope with other challenging feelings. That is normal, but how we respond to our depressed state may not be the healthiest way. The only thing that shopping will do will be to reduce your financial net worth (which then emotionally makes you feel bad) and put you deeper into debt.

Of course you want to look good and you want to feel good – I understand that. However, by no means do we have to take the extremes of killing our budget with overspending or look like we are dressing from another generation by not spending at all.

Credit cards

Boy, do they like to keep you happy! Going on shopping sprees with credit cards is a sure way to keep us "happy" – and keep us in debt. They are very generous with their credit limits and their special offers, anything to keep you hooked and interested for as long as they possibly can. Don't fall for it. Keep one credit card that can be used universally even if you travel overseas and one back-up card in case something happens to the first one. This is particularly important for families with children. Stay away from department store credit cards, gas credit cards, and special offer credit cards. You don't need them. The same places will accept your primary and secondary credit card just the same. Having multiple credit cards will only tempt you even further and cause you to have many, many credit card bills; you will have to spend more time managing the various payments, and thus it will be harder for you to get out of debt.

When should you use your credit cards? There are many different scenarios that I will share with you, and you can pick the option that works best for you.

American Express cardholders can earn points or money that gets put into a high-yield savings account. Basically, for every dollar you spend on your card, 1% is transferred to your savings account. Not bad. Well, in this case since it is free money – go ahead and use your card for as much as you can, provided you pay off the entire balance by the end of the month.

If you know you don't have the money in your budget or the discipline to do that, then cut down on the purchases or do not use your card. Most American Express cards require you to pay the whole amount off by the due date. If you have bad credit or have a bad payment history, this may not be the card for you.

Rewards points are pretty popular with credit cards including American Express, Visa, MasterCard, and Discover card. Most Visa, MasterCard, and Discover credit cards allow you to pay over time. As long as you pay the minimum amount due, and do not exceed your credit card limit, you remain in good standing with them. You can also earn points to redeem in the future (when you've accumulated different increment levels of points) for rewards that range from items to gas and restaurant gift cards to travel vouchers. Again, if you want to earn points and have good paying discipline, use your credit card to earn the points, sky miles or whatever it is they are offering. If you have less than perfect credit and have a hard time paying for whatever reason, then refrain from using your card as much as you can and buy only what you need when you need it – if it is an absolute necessity and you have no cash available.

The reason why it is so important to pay off the entire balance each month is because when you only pay the minimum balance due, and you leave an open balance on your credit card, you are charged interest. Credit card companies earn billions of dollars annually from interest charges alone. Think of how much better it would be to have the money you're spending in interest remain in your pocket and not theirs. Not only that, your credit score is calculated based on the amount you pay towards your monthly balance. Do not expect your credit score to go up by leaps and bounds if you are paying your minimum balances only.

If you have a lot of credit cards (meaning more than five) and you are not planning to buy a house in the near future, make a plan to pay them off and then close three or four of them. The plan you make and your discipline in sticking to it will be crucial to your end results.

It is true that canceling the bulk of your credit cards may lower your credit score temporarily because it can look as though you can't handle credit and so you're getting rid of it. Therefore, if you are planning to purchase a home, car, or any other major item where you will need as much of your credit as possible, pay off the balances but do not close out the cards. That shows your creditors that you *can* handle having credit cards in your possession without running them up to their limits.

Ultimately, however, getting yourself to the point of having only one major credit card and one minor back-up credit card is worth it. In the short-term your credit score will be lowered (slightly), but in the long-term it will be super-charged. I know because I did this myself as part of my "Get out of debt" plan. Purging your credit report of excess credit cards once they are paid off can eliminate you from having to deal with the following:

- The temptation to use them
- Having open balances on your credit cards
- Having to deal with all the statements and paper clutter
- Available credit calculated on your credit report

Even though you might have five credit cards with zero balances, that credit line is still available to you. Therefore, it is still calculated in your credit score because the possibility that you could spend up to that limit is there. In the past eleven years I have canceled over six credit cards and my credit score is pretty high, so I know this plan works. It did take some time to reach this goal, and I did not do this when I was getting ready to buy a home. Be patient and make a plan. Consult with wise, trusted family members who are also good money managers or talk to a trusted accountant. This recommendation takes time and discipline.

Which credit cards to keep and which ones to eliminate?

When I analyzed my credit card extravaganza, I followed a couple of simple rules. Here are some questions to ask yourself as you consider which cards to set aside for keeping and which to eliminate:

- Which credit card offers the best rewards points, miles, cash, benefits, no annual fees, the lowest interest, and the best credit line? Find out which ones and set them aside.

- Which ones are accepted universally, meaning overseas? Most are, but some department store credit cards are limited to your local area. Find out which cards can be used anywhere in the world and set them aside.

- Which credit card gives me the best credit line, meaning a credit line that can cover my family and me in times of a great need, such as a funeral, accident, or medical situation? Amounts vary from family to family, but in my experience, try to have enough credit to be able to cover unexpected funeral costs or a medical emergency.

To be open and honest with you, when a family member of mine passed away we had to scrape and scrounge to pay for the funeral. Nobody had the money to pay for the funeral. I was mortified; furthermore, I felt so frustrated that this happened in our family that I vowed to always have at least that much available to me in credit card lines, if not in ready cash which is the best-case scenario. Don't let this experience happen to you. We should all be able to pass away in peace and with dignity.

Now, pick the credit card with the best perks and highest credit line for your primary credit card. Next, do the same for your secondary credit card. I highly recommend a secondary credit card. You just never know.

Here is something to remember: You cannot withdraw cash from American Express credit cards. You only have access to cash with Visa, MasterCard, and Discover. They provide you with a pin number upon acceptance of your application, which you typically receive before or after you receive your card.

Once you've activated your credit card you can withdraw money from any ATM machine as long as you accept the bank fees for making that withdrawal, which can run anywhere from $1.50 – $2.50 per withdrawal. I am not in the habit of withdrawing money from my credit cards, because you can be charged with high interest fees as well. I would rather use my cash. But, being able to do this could make a big difference for you in case of an emergency.

Which credit card do I recommend?

If you have good credit and good paying habits, I highly recommend American Express. Why? Well, with American Express you are required to pay off the entire balance every month, and that is that! Because you *know* you cannot pay a partial amount, you pay off what you spent, period. It develops discipline and keeps your credit rating in good standing.

Although American Express has now developed a credit card that allows you to make partial payments to reduce your balance, which appeals to a broader audience, I still highly recommend that if you want to get an American Express credit card, get one that requires you to pay off the full balance every month. Develop the discipline to pay well and routinely. Never take for granted the power of your credit card.

They say credit is more powerful than cash. There is much controversy around this statement – but having good credit is essential to your financial health and portfolio well being.

Credit cards are good when they are utilized correctly, and they can make a great statement on even the most powerful and high-profile people in the world. Use them wisely, enjoy life, and remember, never substitute credit cards as a means of paying for your living expenses.

The average credit card holder has about five credit cards to their name and often has credit card balances. Stick to one primary and one secondary card. If you have credit card balances, make a plan to pay them off as soon as possible.

Loans

The loans people take out can vary, and the reasons they take them out can also vary. A car loan is purely for the purchase of a vehicle and you do not receive any cash out of the loan. A standard loan, also known as a signature loan, gives you a set amount of cash. The interest fees vary and the amounts you can get also vary. Each type of loan has a pre-determined number of monthly payments, and the amount of each payment is set from the beginning. Those payments usually begin the very next month.

If you have a car loan and several small loans, don't despair; make a plan to pay them off by paying a little extra on each monthly payment (check to make sure there is no pre-payment penalty fee). Having a solid plan to pay everything off and remain debt free is a worthy goal. It may take some time, so be patient with yourself and try your best to be disciplined in making your payments. Also, in the meantime, try not to take out any more loans than you already have.

Small steps for a big result

Avoid any of the vices mentioned in the previous chapter and maximize the potential of your finances. Use your money wisely; pay your bills on time every month and do not skip a payment. Skipping a payment can cost you a late fee and possibly an over-limit fee if you are already close to the limit on your credit card; each of these fees is usually $30 in most cases, so be careful. Watch your money and avoid any unnecessary purchases. Taking small steps like these can take you far and put you on a path of success. To "keep on keeping on" is what yields great results. Give yourself time and don't get discouraged. Sometimes we feel that we are getting nowhere, especially when it comes to paying off credit cards, when every month we are charged interest. Sometimes it feels like we are taking two steps forward and one step backward, but remember, consistent, steady effort *does* bring results.

Try not to pay only the minimum balance on your credit cards if you can. Make larger than required payments so you can pay the balance off much quicker. Of course, if you can only afford to pay the minimum amount, then do so knowing that it is still accomplishing something of value – you are keeping your payment history current on your credit report (which tracks late payments for seven long years).

When I was in debt, I was determined to get out of debt as quickly and safely as I could. By doing this safely I mean, in addition to paying down the debt, I always paid all of my regular bills such as telephone, cable, electricity, and so on. I always had money for food and I always saved some money. Not much, but I saved something, no matter how little, to help make me feel safe and comfortable. I have always felt like I need to have some money put away in case I got sick or I needed medical help. Even though I had medical insurance, I would still need some money for paying the deductible or for paying my portion of the prescription costs. Since I did not have any supplemental insurance back then, this was something I had to worry about. So, even while paying off my debt, I did my best to juggle paying all my bills and saving some money besides, and I remained hopeful in the meantime.

The infamous loan sharks

Yes, they exist, as I mentioned earlier. They offer unsecured high interest loans. They are dangerous because they know they are most likely many people's last resort for getting access to much-needed funds when they cannot get loans anywhere else because of their poor credit. If you are stuck in one of these loans (commonly called "payday loans"), it is very important to do your best to pay it off as quickly as possible because already, with this type of loan, you are repaying much more than the original loan amount, and stretching it out makes this even worse. On the other hand, paying your bills regularly every month may result in your being able to obtain future loans from a respectable bank if and when you need them.

Why do I mention these loan sharks? Well, because they are out there and many people do have to resort to using them. When all else has failed because your credit is poor – the loan sharks are ready for you. Do you know why they are called loan sharks? Some of them will injure you or your family members if you do not pay. They may even damage your property and steal from you to speed up the loan repayment process. More often than not, the loan sharks exercise their power. They will get their money.

Turning to a loan shark when you're in a financially desperate situation is something that you want to avoid at all costs. Please don't think of them as one of your solutions. They know you are desperate for money and so they come across as your best friend. But, they have a policy – you either pay or you suffer.

Bottom line: keep your bill payments up-to-date and show your respectable lenders you are willing to pay. If you are struggling and know that you won't be able to make a payment on time, call them or write to them and let them know your status and that you fully intend to pay. Many lenders will respect you for communicating with them. Work out a payment schedule with them or suggest one. Most of the time your creditors will be more than willing to work out a plan with you. As long as you keep the monthly payments coming in, they will remain satisfied.

Write a letter to the three credit reporting agencies (Equifax, Experian, and TransUnion) explaining your financial situation. Explain how you ended up in debt, if you feel it is worth letting them know, and explain that you are on a plan to pay everything off. This puts a statement on your credit file that shows any future lender that you are committed to paying your debt. When they see you are a committed payer and you have a plan to get out of debt, then they will review your case differently. It does not guarantee you will get a loan, but it does say something about you. This way, when the lender pulls your credit report and sees your list of debts as well as the statement you've placed as an explanation, they are seeing someone who is working to resolve their financial problems. If they pull your credit report and see a list of debts and no written statement of explanation from you on the file, then they are not sure what you are doing about it or what the whole picture looks like.

If you are in debt, make a plan to pay it all off. Remember, good budgeting and planning will help you. If you are not in debt, that is something to be proud of! However, it is still wise to develop a good budget and keep solid plans to help you stay that way, to stay organized, and to remain at peace.

Budgeting

If you are in debt, a good budget and a good plan will help you get out of debt. While stores are very generous with their discounts to get people into a spending mood, you can benefit from the discounts if there is something you *need* to buy anyway. Just remember to shop with a list and stick with that list!

Let's take a look at some of the important things we need to budget for:

- Housing

- Water
- Electricity
- Telephone
- Home heating (natural gas or oil heat)
- Gasoline for your car
- Insurance
- Food
- Medical Expenses
- Entertainment
- Education
- Home Maintenance
- Children's Allowance (for parents)
- Clothing
- Debt reduction if applicable
- Emergencies (keep money in a separate account)

There could be more, but for the most part these are the general categories families need to budget for. Your budget should ensure that every month you have the money to pay the important necessities to run a household.

Develop a good plan

This may sound funny, but many people actually get high blood pressure when they have to maneuver their way through a really crowded mall, especially after dealing with the hustle and bustle of the parking lots! In my case, I do not have time for dealing with all that. I stick to online shopping. I always find what I am looking for and I am not so tempted to buy more. Many online stores have discounts just like the regular stores at the mall.

Saving time by shopping online can translate into having more time to work to pay your bills off or to spend quality time with your family. Many times when people go to the mall they are there for up to three hours unless they plan to just go in and out of one store, which in most cases does not happen.

Those couple of hours can go towards a second job to help you get out of debt. Using those hours to work can also keep you away from the temptation to buy more "stuff" that you most likely don't need anyway. When we end up going to the mall and seeing this on sale or that on sale, we tend to tell ourselves that it is only a couple of bucks so why not buy it. Well, this kind of thinking can get us in debt and keep us there if we are not careful.

I have friends who are the greatest at finding the best discounts you can imagine! They tell me this shirt was only "this much" or these pants were "only that much." Yet, they are in debt and live paycheck to paycheck. They also have a closet loaded with "stuff". When I try to point this out to them, they insist that is not why they are in debt. Recognizing your habits and developing a great budget plan can help anyone at any stage in their financial journey.

Even wealthy people have budgets, plans, and to-do lists in place before the next day arrives. (In fact, this is most likely how they got wealthy in the first place!) It is important to do this – actually, it is necessary because it helps you keep everything in check and also helps you stick to commitments you have made. A commitment could be a promise you've made to a lender to repay them a certain amount on a certain day of each month. You do not want to forget that promise, especially if you are working hard to get out of debt. The last thing you want to do is give up on a commitment you've made to yourself and your family.

Analyze your budget

Budgeting may not be everyone's favorite thing to do, but it is important. Budgeting helps you make sure you do not overspend and fall into any additional debt, which can happen very easily these days. With all the enticing offers and deals that are going around, it is hard to avoid buying things we want (but don't need).

Keeping a budget and sticking to it helps you keep your money in order and gives you the freedom to spend what you can after careful thought and consideration. Budgeting helps you understand your needs, wants, and the particulars of your basic household needs, and it keeps your money in order.

If things get financially tight and you need to cut back, study your budget and see what you must pay now and what can wait. Many times a trip to the movies, eating out, or a night out on the town will have to wait so you can pay an important bill.

Discipline and wisdom will need to play a strong part in your financial purity portfolio. Get used to understanding your habits and needs so you can learn to plan for them. Discipline yourself to wait on any non-urgent, non-important items like a trip to the movies, for example. Get wisdom so you can understand the ramifications if you end up not paying a bill and instead opted for wasting your money on something "fun" to do. When you are in debt your finances require extra tender loving care. Now is not the time for you to neglect your bills and pay late, especially if you are trying to get out of debt and you have a plan in order with your lenders to work off your debt. If you fail to pay a bill or a loan payment, remember what you will be charged:

- A late fee
- Interest on the unpaid and late balance
- Over-limit fees if your balance is already close to your limit, and the late fee causes your balance to go over the limit (a true catch-22 situation)

And your credit will not get any better but will only get worse, and on and on the cycle will continue ....

Look for ways to save money

Coupons and discounts

A good habit for you to develop is to look for ways to save money. For example, we all need to buy food weekly or monthly, so why not be on the lookout for coupons and discounts?

Many newspapers offer great coupons and discounts. Taking some time every week to cut coupons can help us save money, even enough money to more than make up for the cost of buying the newspaper. Depending on where you live, the majority of the coupons come in the Sunday paper. Take some time to cut the coupons for the products you already buy anyway or having been planning to try. (Don't cut a coupon for something you would normally never buy, because then you are actually causing yourself to spend money you wouldn't normally spend.)

Look through your newspaper, magazines, catalogs, and advertising packets that come in the mail with coupons enclosed, and cut them out right away. (If you set it aside and tell yourself you'll do it later, you most likely won't get around to it.) Buy yourself a little coupon organizer and categorize them by cleaning supplies, meats, dairy, household items, laundry items, and so on. Keep the coupon organizer in your car or purse so it will already be with you when you go to the grocery store.

Many people save hundreds of dollars per year using coupons, and some grocery stores have double coupon discounts on certain days. If you use a coupon for 30 cents it counts as double and is now worth 60 cents – that is something that I would run after. Even if you have only five such coupons you will have saved $3.00. Add all your coupons together to get an idea of how much you will save, and when you are grocery shopping think of what a good job you're doing maintaining your financial purity.

It may take a little time to cut the coupons out, but it is worth it. Newspapers and catalogs go through great lengths to print the coupons and barcodes so you can save money. Take advantage of it. It is your money – protect it.

Teach your children the importance of saving, and how small amounts of money can add up to a lot when combined together. Give them the task of cutting the coupons out. Teach them what to look for and what products you are interested in.

Healthy food as a way to reduce medical expenses

Medical expenses seem to be one of the biggest expenses people have besides their home and food. A very economical way to help combat getting sick is drinking green tea on a regular basis. If you do not want to drink green tea then at least drink it during the cold season when everyone gets sick. It has been proven that green tea is loaded with anti-oxidants that can help your body in numerous ways. It can help fight diseases, keep you from getting sick, and help prevent cavities, to name a few of the health benefits of green tea. I drink it regularly, and I encourage you to consider green tea as a healthy alternative.

Once you get sick, you will need to buy medicine, go see the doctor, lose a day or two from work, and pay your health insurance deductible out of your own pocket if you do no have any supplemental insurance. You might even miss many days of work depending on how sick you are. If you are paid on an hourly basis, you will not be paid for those missed days, which will seriously impact your ability to pay upcoming bills, unless you can use a vacation day. You can save quite a bit of money by helping to keep yourself from getting sick. Let's take a look:

Doctor visit co-pay: $20–$40
Prescription medication: $20–$40 deductable

Over-the-counter cold medicine: $8 – $15
Time away from work: $120 – $350

Cost for year-round green tea: $50 – $60

Does green tea absolutely ensure you do not get sick? No. Is it worth the try to keep you healthy during the cold season? Yes.

Drinking a few cups of green tea every day all year round can help you from getting sick. I think it is worth doing this as a regular practice throughout the year, especially when the weather is cold.

Again, there is no way to absolutely ensure you will not get sick, but the benefits of green tea are grand.

Furthermore, green tea tastes good, and drinking it is a relaxing experience. Try it. Your body will thank you for it.

Dry Cleaners

I know we all have nice clothes that need to be dry cleaned, but taking most of your everyday clothes to the cleaners can be expensive and time consuming, and sometimes is not even necessary. Try to minimize taking clothing to the dry cleaners, especially if you tend to do so because you like the way they press the clothes. Many times, your clothes can be ironed carefully with a good iron. When you shop for clothes you can also look for items that do not need dry cleaning but can easily be washed, dried, and ironed (if necessary) at home. This will save you money, and it will help you avoid making time-consuming trips to the dry cleaners, which is especially important when you have a busy schedule. Remember, not everything HAS to go to the dry cleaners, and probably many of the clothes you are sending to the cleaners can be laundered at home. Let's take a quick look at the best reasons for using dry cleaning:

- Dry clean only for the clothing that requires it based on the notation on the clothing label
- Invest in a good iron to handle any other clothing you want pressed neatly
- Ironing helps you save money – up to $12 per item
- Ironing saves you trips to the dry cleaner, which then saves you time and money spent on the gas it takes to get there

Food shopping

I must confess I do enjoy food shopping. It is a time for me to take a look at the fresh foods that are in season and available and see what kinds of recipes I can create. I love cooking, so naturally I love to go food shopping.

How does food shopping contribute to financial purity? It can do so in many ways. Let's look at a few.....

First, are you cutting out those coupons? If not, then get busy! Enlist your kids to do the task as a way to train them, or if you are simply short on time. Save, save, and save some more money, every chance you get, whenever you can, in anything you buy, anywhere you buy!

Avoid buying junk food

Buying junk food is a very expensive habit to get into and it brings unhealthy food into your home. Do you really want to serve your family food that is low on nutrition and full of empty calories? Junk food does not provide the vital, necessary doses of vitamins and minerals you and your children need to be full of life and to keep from getting sick.

I am a huge fan of homemade cooking and NOT processed foods like frozen dinners. It doesn't matter if I am short on time; I insist there is a healthy recipe out there you can prepare in no time at all.

If you were to do a comparison between families that opt for homemade cooking and families that eat processed foods because they are fast and easy to make, you would see that the family that opts for homemade cooking generally does not get sick as frequently as the family that opts for eating processed food, and fast food.

I have a friend who eats out every day for every meal except breakfast. She eats lunch and dinner out every single day. Let's take a look at her story. She is constantly sick – always sick. She earned her nickname "sickly" very fast. Now let's take a look at how this eating pattern has also affected her finances.

She is constantly in the doctor's office. Last time I checked she was at the doctor's office three times in one month. Even though she has a medical plan she still had to pay her $65 deductible. Because she was often prescribed antibiotics, she would spend another $60–$80 on the prescription medication deductible. It doesn't stop there. She is frequently absent from work because she is sick and the medicine puts her to sleep or makes her groggy, leaving her unable to get to work.

We haven't even touched on the spending she does eating out every day, which has been known to top out at $1,000 per month. Add in the medicine and doctor visits and you now have an expense of over $1300, give or take a few dollars.

Sometimes people do not realize how much money they spend on take-out food or worse yet, the negative effects non-homemade cooking can have on their bodies. They often insist that they make good food choices, such as eating a salad or soup. But the truth is, eating out is eating out. The pots and pans used are different, the ingredients used are different, and many times items are loaded with corn syrup and fatty ingredients that end up being part of your meal whether you would normally eat them or not. When you go food shopping, you have control over what you buy and what you put into the recipes you make. When you eat out, you get what you get, and then you have to pay. Get wisdom into the benefits of nutritious food that you've bought yourself and the joy of cooking. There is a good reason why we all have kitchens. Let's put them to good use!

Even if you are wealthy you may still be striving for financial purity and healthy living. If you can afford to do so, hire a great cook that can make you delicious, healthy homemade meals you can enjoy.

If you are not wealthy, then invest in a great cookbook that offers healthy and fast recipes for you and your family.

Another thing we do not realize is the effect eating out has on our health, not only immediately, but in the long-term. Everything you do now will have an effect on you later on in life. For example, if you go to college now it will help you have a more profitable career later on. If you smoke now, you will deal with the effects of smoking later on.

My friend who eats out every day is also overweight, which causes her to diet constantly, spending money on this diet or that diet pill; it makes me want to cry every time I hear her say she is on another diet. It is almost unbearable for me to endure as she fails to see the vicious cycle she is caught up in.

Let's take a moment to consider once again all the time and the exhaustion spent in going to all the restaurants, doctor's office, pharmacies, being sick in bed, and missing work. If we were to make healthy eating a regular part of our lifestyle we could easily take that time and translate it into time spent at home with the family eating good cooking.

This is much better than being sick and thus having to work another job to pay off your increased bills, which makes it even harder to get out of debt. Eating out should be done occasionally and primarily for a special event of some kind. Watch what you eat, and most of all, watch what you buy with your hard-earned money.

Dieting

The effects of dieting weigh heavily on our bodies even though we may not see it at first. What many people don't realize is that they have slowly been gaining weight due to poor eating habits, and then they try to frantically diet to lose the weight in a short amount of time. When they don't see any results in a matter of days, they switch to another diet and then another, looking for the magical diet that will help them drop the weight NOW. It can take people years to gain weight but they insist on losing the weight instantly. The fortune we spend on special diets, dieting pills, and all dieting related items is appalling. Then people wonder why they are broke and sick.

We should be developing a deliberate, consistent, long-term lifestyle plan (there's our favorite word *planning* again!) that allows us to control our money and preserve our health to the best of our abilities. It can be done.

Knowing the atrocious elements that cause you to be sick and sometimes poor is the first step to developing your financial purity. Keeping yourself healthy is a sure way to walk in the path of financial purity and enjoy life.

Putting our body through constant dieting can shock our body and cause unexplainable stress-related illnesses. I cannot stress enough the dangers of dieting both physically and financially. While some diets and diet pills do help people to lose weight, doing so often comes with a price ranging from $19 to thousands. Many diet pills can cause serious side effects. Many dieting organizations will defend their products as being helpful and healthy, but the truth is that long-term use of these products causes health problems and a constant outpouring of cash from your pockets.

Many of these diets and weight loss programs are short-lived. Most of us simply get off the pill or diet plan because we have lost the weight we desired to lose, and then we go right back to our poor eating habits, which will only lead us back to the weight gain we so dreaded.

Unless you are extremely overweight, please don't diet; see a doctor or nutritionist who can help you with a great nutritional meal plan. Don't go it alone; see a specialist who can help ensure that you are getting all the vitamins and minerals your body needs while avoiding any poor foods for your body.

Making the decision to go food shopping regularly, purchasing wholesome, natural, organic foods, and exercising on a regular basis is the sure and long-term way to keeping healthy, staying fit, and building financial purity. The money you would otherwise spend on diets can remain in your bank account, or you can invest it or use it to tithe ... a godly action.

Are you seeing the elements of financial purity coming together? Are you seeing what makes up financial purity?

Learn to love your life and study your spending habits as often as you can. If you feel you are spending your money unwisely, then analyze your actions. What can you do differently? What can you do to produce higher profits from your hard-earned money? What can you not buy? What should you buy? How should you spend your time? Should you work extra to pay off a bill early or work less to spend more time with your family?

Every person and every family is different. Study what benefits you the best, read the Bible for daily wisdom, and pray over your budgeting and the steps you plan to take to get out of debt. When you have a plan and you are determined to follow it, you will eventually get out of debt. Remember to pray for everything!

Chapter 7

Your Credit Report and Score

Show me your ways, O LORD, teach me your paths. Psalm 25:4

Your credit score is very important to your financial well-being. It measures how you have paid your bills in the past and how you have managed your money. In essence, it is like a school grade or like your grade point average (GPA). It is an indicator of how well you are doing in your finances.

Do you know you credit score? Do you know what your credit report looks like? If you don't, find out. I recommend you obtain a copy of your credit report about four times a year. The easiest way to do this is to pay for a credit score watch service that tells you on a monthly basis what is going on in your finances.

If you have been denied credit, you can get a copy of your credit score for free, but the best-case scenario is to be able to check your credit report and score whenever you want to. You need to be aware of what is on your credit report and what your credit score is. No one should know more about your credit than you, not even your lenders or your bank. You should be the primary, most knowledgeable person when it comes to your credit report and score. Why wouldn't you want to know about such an important part of your life?

All about credit reports and scores

Before we go into detail about credit reports and scores, let's take a moment to look over the following chart. This represents the most commonly used credit score scale among the three credit reporting companies:

Excellent	• 750 - 840
Good	• 660 - 749
Fair	• 620 - 659
Poor	• 340 - 619

Where do you stand? If you are in the fair or the poor range, don't worry, take heart, and cheer up! You can improve! Being in the "good" range is great and you should fight hard to get in the excellent range and stay there.

It is a little unfair, but true, that we are many times judged by our credit score. Conclusions are often made of us as to whether we are a "deadbeat" – meaning we do not pay our bills – or a responsible person. I wish I could tell you this does not happen, but it does. We are labeled based on how good our credit score is. Another thing you should be aware of is that many companies pull credit reports on potential employees who are applying for certain positions. Even they want to see your score.

I have known Christian men and women refuse to date someone with bad credit no matter what the circumstances were that got them into that situation. I cannot stop people from making harsh judgments about others, but I can exhort people to improve their scores. The fastest and easiest way to improve your score is to start making a plan to pay everything off.

Believe it or not, Christians are often "expected" to have good credit. Well, we are all human and things happen. Should we leave things as they are? No. We should always strive to improve and get better no matter what our circumstances are.

Another thing you can do is refrain from sharing your situation with everyone if you feel you are being judged unfairly. If you know that certain people are harsh critics, stay away from them during this time of debt reduction. Being around them will only discourage you and make you feel bad. Do stay close to the people who encourage you, lift you up, and help you to remain on target. If it helps, find a mentor or an accountability partner.

If you fall into the category of Poor credit with a score of 340 – 619, here is what you can do to improve it:

- Sign up for a monthly credit score watch service.
- Look over your updated credit report several times a year.
- Get familiar with your finances. Comb through your credit report.

- Is everything accurate, and do all the accounts listed belong to you?
- Make a plan to pay everything off
- Get busy writing a letter to the credit agencies explaining your situation
- Remain cheerful – your score can go up

If you fall into the category of Fair credit with a score of 620-659, here is what you can do:

- Sign up for a monthly credit score watch service
- Look over your updated credit report several times a year
- Get familiar with your finances. Comb through your credit report.
- Is everything accurate, and do all the accounts listed belong to you?
- Make a plan to pay off whatever you can
- Pay everything on time, including your utility bills
- Be patient; you score will go up

If you fall into the category of Good credit with a score of 660-749 here is what you can do:

- Sign up for a monthly credit score watch service
- Look over your updated credit report several times a year
- Is everything accurate, and do all the accounts listed belong to you?
- Pay everything on time, including your utility bills
- Are there any accounts you can pay off and then close?

If you fall into the category of Excellent credit with a score of 750-840, here is what you can do to maintain it:

- Sign up for a monthly credit score watch service
- Look over your updated credit report several times a year
- Continue to do what you are doing
- Teach others what you have done
- Remain up-to-date on everything you have

It is vital to keep a close eye on your credit report and score. Start by purchasing your credit report and score. Then, get on a credit score watch service, which you can purchase at the same time you purchase your credit report. This usually costs about $10–15 per month, which is worth every penny because it allows you to know the status of your credit report and score at any time.

You can easily do this by going online to one of the three major credit organizations: Equifax, Experian, and TransUnion. All three websites are secured, and you can easily purchase both your credit report and your credit score at the same time. You can buy your credit report from either one of the credit organizations or you can buy all three together at the same time, which is what I recommend. Equifax and Experian go back all the way to when you started building your credit; TransUnion may not go back that far.

You now have the option of purchasing a three-in-one credit report and credit score. Be sure to purchase your credit score and credit score alert. I believe this is a small price to pay for such valuable information, which provides you with peace of mind. If something goes wrong, then you can identify and correct it quickly. Be in the know.

As I mentioned, the credit reporting agencies' website are secure. There are a select group of questions that only you can answer before the purchase is complete. If there are any hints or doubts that the person accessing your file may not be you, then the purchase cannot be completed. Much effort has been put into making the websites accurate, secure, safe, and easy to use. Be in the know and get a copy if your credit report and credit score, even if you request it via mail.

When you sign up for a credit watch service you are emailed once a month with your credit score. You can see if your score has gone up or gone down. If your score has changed, they will give you an explanation of the reason for the change. Some of the most common occurrences that will cause your score to change are the following: you paid off an account; you took out another loan or credit card; you fell behind in your payments on an account; or, some new activity transpired on your account within the past 35 – 45 days.

As you can see, this is a great tool to have at your disposal. You can really keep track of what is going on. You can also see what causes your score to go up or down. You can also see if something shows up on your credit report that you did not authorize, and then you can take action.

Opened up a new account? Paid one of your major bills late? All this will affect your credit score by several points, depending on what you have done over the past 35 – 45 days. All of your creditors report your payment behavior every 30 days. It takes approximately 15 days after that for it to be reflected on your credit report accordingly. Be diligent and watch what you do. Your credit score indicator is an excellent start to understanding your financial behavior.

Good reasons to know your credit score:

- To help you stay focused on getting out of debt so that you can improve your score.
- To keep a close watch and thus avoid being the victim of identity theft.
- To simply be in the know about your finances.

Credit reports and credit scores are strictly based on your debt and payment history. Your score is not based on how much money you have in the bank, although that factor may be considered when you are applying for a home loan. Your income is also not reflected on your credit report, but it will be considered whenever you apply for any type of loan.

Many times when I talk to people about the importance of monitoring their credit reports and scores, I ask them how often they look at them. Most people reply that they only check if they are planning to make a large purchase. They say that they either do not care to know or are afraid to purchase them online.

Many people also tell me that they are not obsessed about their money and desire to live day by day. There is a huge difference between being obsessive and being responsible and aware of your credit information. You *do* need to know what is on your credit report, and it is not about being obsessive, even if you purchase it several times a year, which is what I recommend. You are being responsible and aware in wanting to obtain your information firsthand, because doing this allows you to correct any errors quickly if there are any. It also tells you how you are doing overall, and what your various credit accounts are doing to your financial well-being. Certain websites even have little reports you can utilize that help you determine what you can do to improve your credit score. They offer fantastic advice and most importantly, you know everything about your financial record. Nothing is a secret, and nothing is a mystery. This prevents you from having to say the embarrassing phrase, "Really, is that all that's in there? I didn't know ..." to a creditor you are trying to borrow money from. Be intelligent, and be prepared to anticipate any questions your creditor may ask you.

Study what is on your report

You will get detailed information about your personal information, credit history, or collections if you have them. Study your report. Get familiar with your financial standing. Make sure personal information is accurate and that all the accounts listed really do belong to you.

Be sure that you are aware of everything on your report

Mistakes on credit reports happen all the time. They are more common than you think. The credit bureaus are not going to fix them voluntarily; *you* have to identify the mistakes and notify the credit agencies, and then they will correct the errors. If you do not correct the mistakes on your credit report they can stay on there for years causing your credit report to be inaccurate and possibly hurt your score. That is why it is so important for you to get your credit report on a regular basis. Get out of the mentality that you are being obsessive about your money and stop being afraid. The websites are very secure. It is even more important to get your credit score alert monthly. You can know of a change within days of it happening. The power of knowing your credit report and score in today's atmosphere of proliferating identity theft cannot be overstated, especially when that information is readily available to you with the click of a button. Click away!

If there are mistakes, make arrangements to get them corrected

You can do that by initiating a dispute online. If you are not able to do this, all credit bureaus have an address on their website where you can write to them and let them know of the mistakes you've found on your report. You will need to provide your personal information and supporting documents of what you are disputing. For example, you may have canceled an account or a credit card and your report shows that it is still open. You would provide them with the date you closed the account, confirmation number if you have one, or a confirmation letter you might have received from the credit card company or bank. You would do the same thing for any other discrepancies you may have found. Ask for a new copy of your corrected updated credit report and that you want it resolved in thirty days. They are normally very good about resolving disputes within thirty days unless they need more time to investigate, and in that case, they will notify you via regular mail. Give them thirty days to fix the problem, notify you, and send you a corrected credit report.

Credit clutter

If you have excessive credit cards and loans, decide what you can pay off and when. You do not want to have pages and pages of different credit cards on your credit report. You only need two credit cards, one primary and one secondary in case of an emergency. Some people have several major credit cards, several department store credit cards, and gas cards. Some people have up to twenty credit cards. Again, you only need two. If you have a large number of credit cards and owe money on all of them, get busy paying them off. Once they are paid off, get busy canceling them. Canceling them affects your debt ratio and could bring your score down for a short period of time. I do not recommend doing this if you are in the process of purchasing a home or a vehicle. Wait until your mortgage or car loan is finalized and then get busy paying down debt and closing accounts. This is what I call removing credit clutter and keeping yourself financially pure. You *really do not* need to have credit cards in excess.

Study the loans you have. One? Two? Three? Get busy paying them off. If possible, see about consolidating them for the sake of eliminating the amount of accounts you have open. The amount you owe may remain the same; you would just have one loan instead of several. If you are not able to do this, then stay focused on paying them on time and paying them down. If you can, make larger payments then the monthly amount.

What if you have no debt but you still want to raise your credit score?

Paying your bills on time every time is the first step you can take. Refrain from taking out any new loans, because every time a bank obtains your credit report, your score can go down a couple of points. Your score will go up again as long as you keep paying your bills on time and do not allow any of your accounts to fall into collection or become late.

If you do not have any credit card debt, how can you have a collection show up on your credit file? If you get behind on your phone bill or your cell phone bill by three or four months, not only will they disconnect your service, but they will hand your account over to a collection agency for handling. This can happen to any one of your utility bills if you fail to pay. So pay on time and refrain from taking out any new loans unless you need them.

Better interest rates

A great credit report and score can earn you better interest rates, because lenders see you as low risk and know that you pay well. You can receive a good interest rate on a mortgage or a vehicle loan, and you can even receive a low-interest-rate loan! So why not strive to have a great credit report and score? Go for it and then enjoy the benefits. Work hard at your credit report and manage your money wisely. Your credit report is crucial to your financial well-being and will follow you around no matter where you go.

Keeping it simple

Sometimes, we like to have things just to have things, whether we need them or not. We always want the next best thing, the better car, the upgrade, the bigger house, the shinier watch ... and on and on our desires go.

However, keeping things simple can take us a long way. Do you really need that new car? Why not work towards ownership of the one you have? Why trade it in? What is wrong with owning a car? Why do we have to go into a lease just so we can keep on getting a new car every year or so?

I am not advocating not enjoying whatever you're comfortably able to buy, but I *am* advocating simplicity. Sometimes it is good to restrain ourselves and only buy things when we need them and not just because we want them.

If you're buying another car because you need a bigger car because there has been an addition to your family, that is a good reason for making this purchase decision, or if your old car has broken down to the point of not being worth repairing, that is a valid reason to purchase another vehicle. But there are many people who rush out to get a new vehicle because they just HAVE to have it and they want it. Impulse purchases for big-ticket items such as a new car can weigh heavily on your credit score. Buy what you need when you need it, and be patient with yourself.

Take full responsibility for your debt

You cannot remove any accounts from your credit report that rightfully belong to you. You can dispute something if you see an error in the way it's being reported, but if it is yours (meaning one of your credit cards, your loan, your collection), it will stay there until you pay it off. What is yours is yours. Take full responsibility for your debt and do something about it. Make a plan to pay off your debt completely. Remember, if you dispute something, make sure you have the supporting documents to speed up the resolution process.

Many small steps produce big results. How much time will it take to pay off your debt and improve your score? Everyone's situation is different. There is really no set timeframe because it all depends on how much you're paying every month. The more you're able to pay, the quicker you'll see those balances get reduced. The best way to keep a close eye on this process is to get a copy of your credit report on a regular basis, the sooner the better!

Let's recap...

- Purchase your credit report and your credit score. Get over your fears that the credit agency's website is not secure. Honestly acknowledge to yourself that studying your credit is not being obsessive, but instead is being responsible.
- Study your credit report and get familiar with it.
- Make sure that every account listed on it is yours.
- Quickly dispute any errors by providing supporting documents.
- Eliminate credit clutter.
- Learn what makes your score go up and

down.

- Keep things simple.
- Know how important a good credit rating is in your life.
- If you have debt, develop a plan to get out of debt.
- Keep paying your bills on time to maintain good credit.

Honor God with wisdom in managing your money. Keep things simple to avoid possible complications in the future. Try to avoid feeling envy when you see someone with a new car that you've always wanted or the bigger house you do not have. God will reward you with what He knows is just right for you when He sees fit to do so. Be patient, be wise, remain in prayer, and read the Bible, which is full of scriptures on how to handle money wisely so as to experience financial purity.

Chapter 8

Saving Money

Steady plodding brings prosperity; hasty speculation brings poverty. Proverbs 21:5

How do I increase my profits with what I am doing? Or, what do I need to change to help increase my profits? Asking yourself these questions will lead to peace, organization, joy, and best of all, you will be honoring God with your time *and* with your money, which is something we all strive to do. In this chapter I will describe a simple system that I have implemented into my life, which has given me tremendous freedom.

Poverty mentality

Sadly, many people have developed a poverty mentality, and they have a hard time getting out of this negative way of thinking, which is like a downward spiral that actually leads to poverty. Because they think they are poor, whenever they have to weather even a small financial crisis they are convinced they do not have money and that they will *never* have money. If you have been trapped in a poverty mentality, let me encourage you – the things you've been telling yourself are **not true**! Your past does not dictate your future. Just because your family did not have much money when you were growing up and you went through some difficult times does not mean that you will never have any money at all ever or that you will continue to be in your current difficult situation forever.

Because this is a *mentality* that does not have to reflect your *reality*, you need to train yourself to think you are only going through the situation temporarily and that you **can** get out of it and improve your finances in the long-term. It takes time and it takes work; it takes diligence and faith. You will need to change your thinking little by little so that you are working towards changing your future.

Don't let yourself get mired in worry and don't dwell on the past. Resolve to fix whatever aspect of your finances needs attention, such as getting out of debt, for example. If you have debt, set yourself a goal to pay it off and then move on to greater wealth. Don't stay trapped in your mindset. Why should you think you will never have great wealth or great abundance?

Why save?

There are many reasons why we should save a portion of our earnings, but there are three reasons primarily: we should be saving for our own personal gain, for emergencies, and for future financial freedom. Even though you may be tempted to utilize all your earnings to pay down debt (beyond what you need to pay your regular bills), saving should be one of your top priorities as well.

> **Tithing, paying off debt, and saving have a place in your financial purity portfolio.**

What if you have an emergency, and you have no available credit to use because you are completely up to the limits on your credit cards, and you have no savings to fall back on? What if there is a death in the family and no one has the money to pay for the funeral? What if you do not have friends to help you? Then what do you do?

That is why saving is so important. Put money away every time you get paid and leave it there. I recommend you have a separate savings account just for this purpose. Try not to keep your savings in the same accounts you have for paying the bills and tithing.

Any fears you might have towards saving should be put aside. It's wise to have money tucked away for the future, just for spending on a rainy day, or for something big you are looking forward to, such as a vacation. There is great value in saving and protecting your future.

How to save?

Save something every time you get paid. Steady plodding will take you a long way; you just have to remember it's a step-by-step journey. Saving takes work, discipline, and resistance to not dip into your account when you suddenly want to splurge on an impulse purchase for the latest thing, whatever it is (and something will always come along to tempt you to veer off course).

Below I have outlined some steps you can take to begin saving and organizing your finances. These are steps that have worked for many people and they can work for you too.

Action steps

Most banks will let you open up several different accounts for free, and you can also name them according to their purpose, and choose different debit card and check designs for each one so that you can distinguish between them easily.

Most employers can perform direct deposits for up to five different accounts. Take advantage of this convenience and allow your employer to do it for you. It keeps you organized, and it ensures that setting aside money for saving and for tithing is automatically done for you. All you have to do is fill out a form that provides your employer with the details of each of your bank accounts (such as routing number and account number) and what portion of your paycheck you want to go to each, and they will do the deposits for you.

Here are some steps that have worked for other people, and these can work for you, too. The first step is to open an account for each category mentioned below. If you are short on time, you can easily open up these accounts online. (Check to see which banks allow accounts to be opened up online.) Search out a bank that you are comfortable with and then proceed to open up the accounts. If you have them already, then super! If you are worried about paper and account reconciliation, no worries: many banks now email you your statement at your request. Account reconciliation or check balancing, when updated regularly, can be done online very quickly.

Using this method organizes your finances and ensures that necessary deposits and savings are being done on each payday. Many people say they are disciplined enough to sort of mentally set aside certain amounts of money for saving and tithing within one checking account, but in my experience I have found that it's the rare individual who really achieves this goal. Because all your money is mixed in together, it is easy to find things to spend it on, even if those things are worthy causes such as paying bills and paying down debt. Eventually you'll realize that you have once again forgotten to save anything out of your last check and you have nothing "left over" for tithing or saving.

Have an account for every category and you will find it much easier to keep monitoring your spending, saving, and tithing. If you use direct deposit for each one of these accounts, you will never forget to set aside money for these worthy goals, because those deposits are done automatically.

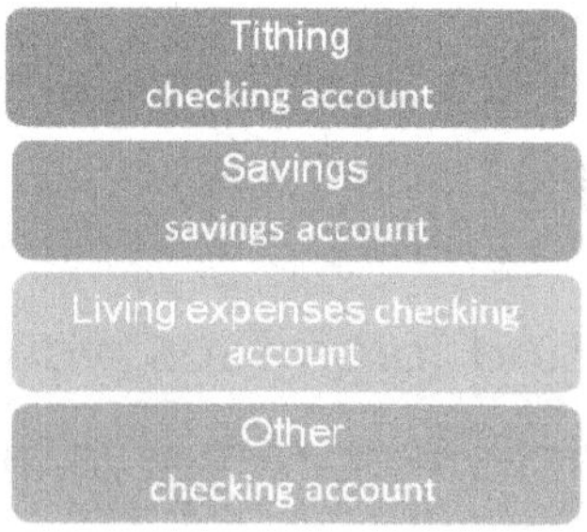

Tithing account

This is the account where your tithes are deposited. The Bible instructs that we should tithe ten percent of our income. Remember, tithing is not about having money to "give away;" it is about being obedient with your money, following God's instructions so you can be blessed. What you do with little things you can do with big things. It is not about the money; it is about the state of the heart.

If you are not tithing already, it is time you start giving according to God's way.

> *I am faithful, so I will abound with blessings. Proverbs 28:20*

Savings account

This is the account where your savings should be deposited. While I do recommend you consistently and diligently save, meaning you don't miss a single payday, how much you save is entirely up to you. Factor in your situation. Do you have debt you are trying to pay down? How much can you put away while still being able to pay all your regular monthly bills? Regardless of how much it is, continue to save something. Maybe you can save ten, fifteen, or even twenty percent.

Living expenses

This is the account where all your money for paying the bills is deposited. This is the remaining amount that is left to be deposited after your tithes and savings have been taken out and deposited into their accounts.

Other account

If you are trying to save for something else or you want a separate checking account for entertainment or whatever it may be, you can certainly do that. The same thing applies if you want to save for something like Christmas or a vacation; you can use a separate account for that too.

Because you are opening many accounts, make sure they are free (meaning you are not charged monthly fees for keeping the account open) and that they do not require you to keep a minimum balance. Check with your employer to see how many direct deposits they can do for you.

Retirement account

Today, many employers offer a retirement account. Are you signed up? If not, then get busy! This is one of the best ways to save for your future. Plus, many employers will match whatever amount you put into the fund. Get familiar with what your employer may offer. I cannot stress enough the importance of having a retirement account for your future.

When you sign up for this retirement account, you will specify the percentage you want to deposit into it from each paycheck. It will come out of your paycheck and get deposited into your account just like how your savings and your tithes are done. If you are tight on money and you have debt you need to pay off, start small, but the main thing is to get started! Get your retirement account established and prepare yourself for the future.

If your employer does not offer a retirement account, then go to your bank and open up your own retirement account. Your financial adviser or a bank manager can help you determine the best option for you. Your bank can even do a direct deposit from your primary checking account to your retirement account so that you do not have to worry about all those deposits. They can make it automatic and easy for you. You just simply fill out a form and they will take care of the rest for you. It is that simple, and the results of your steady work and diligence will be rewarding.

Spending

We all like to spend and indulge ourselves on the things we enjoy. There is nothing wrong with that as long as there is a good sense of balance and moderation. Spending can get out of hand and quickly lead us into debt. If you are trying to pay off debt, then a shopping spree this weekend is out of the question. If you have $500 for the week, then buying a $1,000 item may not be the wisest thing to do. This is how people fall into debt. You need to be watchful over your money; at any given moment you need to know how much debt you have, how well you are doing in paying everything off, and how much you are saving.

Financial purity is not overspending your money, and not spending it on dishonorable items. It is about managing it well, saving, growing it, enjoying it, and honoring God with your tithes. There is a balance, and there is a formula.

If your weakness is shopping and spending in general, no matter what it is you're buying, then try to remove yourself from situations where those weaknesses will be tempted. If going to the mall causes you to whip out your credit card, then don't pay a visit to the shopping mall. If browsing through your favorite catalog is another one of your weaknesses, then cancel that catalog. If you are in the habit of eating out, then try cooking and eating at home. The point is to strive for balance and moderation in everything you do. Pray that God will turn your weaknesses into strengths so that you can refrain from overspending.

Insurance

Insurance is very important to every individual and family. We almost cannot live without it. While there are many different kinds of insurance, below is a list of recommended insurance policies you should have:

- Home insurance
- Car insurance
- Health insurance
- Supplemental insurance
- Life insurance
- Cancer insurance
- Accident insurance
- Short-term disability insurance
- Long-term disability insurance
- Umbrella policy

Some of these are available through your employer but many are not. In many instances, cancer insurance and accident insurance are not covered through your employer. I recommend that you ask your employer how you can buy these policies or if they can offer them through your work, or ask your bank for some good recommendations and check them out. Many banks are well aware of great companies that offer these policies, and many times they offer them as well. My belief concerning insurance is that you can never have enough. You just never know what will happen in life, but if you have all these policies in place, you can know that you are safe and covered.

Most insurance policies are very affordable and almost anyone can get insurance, so price should not be a problem. It is a great investment to have, and it gives you tremendous peace of mind.

Waste

Don't waste your money. Try and save as much money as you can and refrain from spending your money on frivolous items that do not matter or that are hurting you. Wasteful spending can mean different things to different people, but we all have a good sense of what waste is. So be careful what you spend your money on and be careful what you don't spend your money on. For example, not having the proper insurance can be a problem for many families, especially when an accident or an illness occurs. Finding the money to pay for necessary medical bills can be a challenge.

Excess spending on junk items and things of non-importance needs to be put behind you, and you need to start fresh by looking at your money in an entirely different way. It takes work, studying, and creativity to grow your money. Wasting your money is not a way to do that. Here are some steps you can take to avoid waste:

- When you see a penny on the ground, pick it up! (You can clean them later!) Pennies are lying on the ground in abundance. When you add many together they can count for a lot.
- Put all your loose change in a jar to deposit later.
- Avoid constantly eating out. Save it for special occasions.
- Instead of eating lunch out with friends, bring your lunch. You can easily save over $120 a month by making this one simple change.
- Do you *really* need all those magazine subscriptions?
- Do you *really* need to go to that store sale this weekend?

You can ask yourself many questions and study your habits to see how you can eliminate wasteful spending. Little by little everything adds up, and you can end up not having any waste in your finances.

Saving

> *The wise man saves for the future, but the foolish man spends whatever he gets.* **Proverbs 21:20**

Saving is an important step in your financial purity portfolio. Remember, even if you are in debt or do not make that much money, you can still save something, even if it is a little. A little over time goes a long way. The great diligence you put forth now can benefit you later on in life. Think ahead of what you're saving for in your near future, and think of the long-term future as well.

Build a formula that works for you and your family. The formula that works for one family may not work for another, so study what your needs, limitations, and preferences are and make your own formula that fits into your financial purity portfolio.

Let's recap...

- Set yourself free from the poverty mentality
- Always save some money, no matter how little
- Open separate accounts for organizing your money for savings, tithes, and bill paying
- Remember to tithe
- Invest in your retirement account
- Get insurance coverage
- Avoid wasteful spending
- Build a savings formula that works for you

Saving is crucial to our financial well being; it is even mentioned in the scriptures. Your financial purity portfolio will prosper because of it. Take heart; don't be consumed by fear, and trust God when He says that saving is important. He is the Almighty Lord, wise in all things, and His instructions are for the welfare of our finances. Trust God and take action.

Chapter 9

Teaching Children About Money

Show me your ways, O LORD, teach me your paths. Psalm 25:4

Teaching children about money is one of the greatest things we can do to ensure their future financial well-being. I believe children are very sophisticated and deserve to be taught about money as early as possible. We should not treat this as an "adult" topic, because one day they will have to manage their money, and that day comes soon. Many teens get their first job when they're sixteen. Then what? The first thing most teens want to do with their paycheck is spend it as fast as they earn it. Do you think they will learn money management in school? Do you think they will learn good money management skills automatically? The answer to both questions is No, they won't. Don't assume – take action. Teaching children about money can begin as early as when they start doing chores around the house. I have also seen training happen earlier.

It all depends on when you feel comfortable with the topic and how eager your child may be to learn more about money beyond just spending it, such as saving and tithing. It can actually be, very fun to teach children, because they are like sponges; they take in everything you teach them, and I love it! Here is an overview of what children can learn when you intentionally, deliberately, and consistently teach them about money:

- Basic concepts about money
- Responsibility about money
- How to pay the bills
- What not to spend money on
- Do's and don'ts
- Credit reports
- Bank accounts
- Saving
- Investing
- And so much more...

A good training system can help a child manage his or her own money early on with wisdom and experience. Plus, they feel like an adult (what every child wants to be), and they feel like a part of the family decision making. It gets them ready for life.

Parents

You can have your children start managing their money and building their own financial purity from early on. When they're older teens you can have them manage their money by giving them their own credit card with a limit which they will be delighted to have. You can even give them a mini-money class that talks about all the basics and teaches them things they do not learn in school. As I mentioned earlier, money management is very important, and the sooner you start teaching your children, the better they will be at handling their finances when they are out from under your wings. Plan to have time carved out of your schedule, whether monthly or weekly, to teach them some basic financial management. It will be one of the biggest investments in their lives. Here is how they will benefit from the training you give them:

- A good understanding about money

- How to manage their money
- How to balance their checkbook
- How to understand their credit card
- How to pay off their credit card
- The importance of saving
- The value and necessity of baying bills on time

Not only will they benefit from what you teach them, but they can also teach their friends the same principles and be an example to them. The effects of your teaching can touch many people's lives. The important thing is that you get your children inspired and excited to want to learn so that when they're young adults they'll be well equipped to manage their own money.

While they're young you can get creative and assign them tasks. You can give them a project to do, assign them a budget, and encourage them to execute the project with your supervision.

I know a couple who assigned a unique project to their children (who were under the age of eighteen at the time) – to manage the project of removing the carpet from the entire house and installing hardwood floors. They gave their children some rules to follow, a budget to follow, and told them some things they should not do. The children were paid a previously agreed upon amount once the project was finished. It was very interesting to watch how they did it. The results were very good, and seeing this big project through to completion made the children feel like they were truly part of the family. It taught them how to manage a project from start to finish, including managing an operating budget, and they learned how to go about pleasing their parents, a valuable skill that one day will translate into being excellent employees who can successfully manage projects and please their employers.

You may not want to assign a project of this magnitude to your children, but you can give them something that can help them learn the basics of money management. Many parents have limited thinking in terms of what they believe their kids can and cannot do, but the truth is, if you've taught them the right way to do things, you have to put some faith in them and let them test out their knowledge and abilities. If they make a few mistakes, be patient and retrain them; this is how we all learn, and when they do not do something right, you can use that as a teaching experience.

There may be no "right age" when it comes to teaching your child about money. The earlier the better, but whenever you are comfortable doing so you should start. Don't wait for them to ask you to teach them things, because they may never ask. Get them excited and get creative about different ways to teach them valuable skills.

Getting started

As I mentioned earlier, your excitement about teaching money management will drum up their enthusiasm and willingness to learn. If you have only one child, you can suggest that they invite a friend over to be their learning buddy, with the consent of the child's parents, of course. If you have several children then a group session will be great. If you are starting for the first time and there are different ages among the kids in your group, that is no problem. Just simply teach at a level that represents the mid-range age of your group.

Start simple and work your way up to more advanced instruction. Don't skip a step until all the children are confident they understand and have a good handle on the information you're presenting to them.

Explain to the children why it is so important to learn at a young age how to handle money successfully. Talk about how debt is on the increase, and point out how debt has a direct correlation with poor money management.

Teach your children to be wise about money. As they hear things in the news about the financial crisis and the economy, they might have the natural reaction of being afraid even though they don't know what they're afraid of. Teach them that what is going on in the world today does not have to happen to them. Teach and demonstrate to them that you are the master of your money and not its slave, and that they can be the same as well when they begin earning their own money.

Instead of being afraid, some older kids and teens tend to be too relaxed about the topic of money. They are very laid back, casual, and careless about it all – a sort of "whatever" mentality. There is nothing wrong with being relaxed if you're feeling that way because you're handling your money wisely, but that doesn't happen automatically. Responsibility, wisdom, and good counseling are necessary, important, and crucial.

Allowances for children

Start early – the earlier the better! Get your children used to good habits so those habits do not die out quickly. Children should start managing their money from an early age. I am a firm believer in this as well as in the necessity of instilling excellent work ethics in them. The earlier this training begins the better; I cannot stress it enough. As I mentioned previously, schools do not offer money management classes, so you as a parent or guardian need to take up the lead. Don't worry; it will be fun, and it will do your child a lot of good.

Something you can do is to acquire a checking account for your child so they can learn to balance their checkbook on their own. The best way for your child to practice is with his or her own checking account. This will tell your child that you are serious about teaching them the basics of managing their finances.

Something to keep in mind is, depending on your child's age, you may not be able to open a checking account as quickly as you could for an adult. It may require you to speak to the regional branch manager about your plans so they can ensure you will have a smooth experience.

When your child acquires his first checking account it is a big step! The account should also be accompanied with a debit or credit card for teaching purposes so that he can learn how to handle that too.

Once your child has his or her own checking account, you can now use it for teaching. Some basic steps you can start with are the following:

- How to balance the checking account
- How to make a deposit
- How to make a withdrawal
- Understanding the rules of the account

Now that your child has her own allowance and checking account you can teach your child to take care of the items in your budget that are exclusively for them. Instead of you the parent paying for all of these items directly from your budget, why not simply give the money to your child to manage and pay for on their own? You are going to pay for these things anyway, so why not use the paying of these bills and expenses as a teaching experience. Worried? Good! All the more reason why you should stand by their side, supervise and teach, gently and with experience. Talk to them, share with them, but let your children know that they matter and you want them to be the best money managers they can possibly be. Be patient and loving. This will encourage your children to ask questions and not be afraid to make a mistake. Here is a list of the most common items that could be handled from your son or daughter's checking account, since these directly relate to what matters to them in their young lives:

- Cell phone bill
- Pet expenses
- Clothes

- Entertainment expenses
- Lunch money
- Tithing
- Any other expenses they might have

The purpose of your children managing their own checking account, under your supervision, is to teach them the basics of money management. Learning the basics early on can be very beneficial to their future financial well-being, because their habits will be well defined and naturally ingrained within them.

Does this mean your children will end up being wealthy in their adult years? No one can say for certain. Does this mean they will not make any mistakes? No. Does this mean they will have questions about their money management in the future? Absolutely! But it will get them started on a good path having general knowledge of money management. Many kids do not know how to manage a checking account or even get one until they get their first job when they are older teens. Take a different path with your child.

Great money management also leads to great decision making. Great decision making at an early age can help your child make the future decision of whether to buy a $50,000 car or a $5,000 car. Student loans have been known to be as high as $200,000. Helping your child develop good money management skills can also help them understand healthy risk and unsafe risk.

You might be thinking that allowing your children to manage this much money will be a little tricky, because you worry that they will go crazy. True, this could happen – but that is where your supervision as a parent/leader comes in. Here are some rules parents can establish for their children:

- Tithe first
- Set aside money in savings
- Pay for their own lunch
- Pay the bills that have been assigned to them
- Do not allow account to get overdrawn
- If it does, the overdraft fees will come out of next month's allowance
- Clothes and entertainment expenses

come last

- Balance the checkbook every month and show parents

You can develop your own set of rules that are good for both you and your children. Start small if it is comfortable for you, but start somewhere and remember to be patient and understanding. They are just beginning to learn.

An agreement you might have to make with the bank when you open up a checking account for a minor is that you will link it to your own account in the event your child overspends and incurs any overdraft fees. The overdraft fees would them come out of your account (and out of their allowance next month!).

Teach your children about security and the importance of privacy. These are some of the rules your child can follow on a daily basis:

- Do not discuss allowance with friends
- Do not discuss checking account details with friends
- Checkbook remains hidden and private, and

check balancing register is to be updated regularly with each use

- ATM will only be used with adult supervision
- Bank statements are to be organized and filed by date
- Parents are to sign off on their child's account reconciliation and monitor their spending and bill paying
- Credit card will have a very small limit and can only be used for teaching purposes
- Credit card is not to be brought to school
- Bank statements are not to be brought to school
- No online purchases without the consent of a parent or credit card will be suspended for sixty days.
- Any other purchases not on the approved list need to have the parents' approval first.

Points and rewards system

Some credit cards are notorious because of the points and rewards systems they offer their customers. You can adapt this system or implement something similar to motivate, encourage, and stimulate your child's creativity. Why creativity? Because this will motivate them to get busy earning money and learning business skills at an early age.

These systems are brilliant, I think. When fully and properly developed according to your family's budget and needs, using these processes can be an excellent learning experience for your children. They will feel included in the real world; they will feel like an adult (which is crucial in their teen years) and thus will be motivated to do things around the house because they'll see that as an earning opportunity.

Here is an example of one family's reward system that worked beautifully until their child went off to college:

- Cleaning the kitchen - $5
- Taking the garbage out - $1
- Cleaning the bathroom - $3
- Sweeping - $3
- Mopping - $3
- Dusting - $2
- Laundry - $2

- Mowing the lawn - $5
- Requests on demand - $1 – $5

Once you determine your list, if this is something you want to implement, then you can present it to your children. Remember, a parent should always sign off on the activities when they are completed so there is no confusion come the end of the month on pay day.

A frugal child will take full advantage of any extra money they can make. In one family, one child took full advantage of the system and the other one took just enough advantage to buy extra goodies they wanted.

Children in today's world are extremely sophisticated, and this is another way to sharpen their skills and develop them for their young adult years when they'll be out of your house and on their own. Their future independence is just ahead of them and will be here before you know it.

Another good tool to use in teaching money management is to have your children read books on the subject. There are some good books designed particularly for children that you might want to consider providing for them. Remember, the sooner you start teaching your children about money, the better it will be for them.

When you put forth the effort required to teach your child about money early on, you can learn the habits of your children and you can use them for training and correction. If they end up doing something wrong or doing something without your consent, then you can correct them and teach them what they did wrong.

Here is a recap of why you should start teaching your children about money from an early age:

- Schools do not focus on money management classes
- Your children will learn the basics of money
- They will learn how to balance their checking account
- They will learn how to earn money
- They will learn the power of interest
- They will learn the power of compounding
- They will learn the power of hard work
- They will learn the power of entrepreneurial

skills

- They will learn how to stay out of debt
- They will learn the ins and outs of credit card management
- They will learn not to "keep up with everyone else" but instead to stay focused on their own financial plan
- They will learn what to do
- They will learn what not to do
- They will learn to save
- They will learn how to accumulate money
- They will build great wealth habits
- You can teach what you know, right now

You might even learn some valuable new skills while teaching your children!

Another great thing to have your children start doing is learning about investments and savings. Why not? Nothing is too complicated for children to learn because their minds are like sponges. They can participate in seminars, take courses online, and take classes outside of the regular school setting. The point is that you should be constantly teaching your precious and beautiful children something about money. I insist this will help them manage their money without fear, and they will progress further in life sooner than they would without this valuable training.

At the time of writing this book, student loans lead the nation's largest type of debt, followed by revolving debt, including credit cards, and installment loans, including car loans. But student loans lead the pack. These loans are usually the financial burden of students who are only 18 – 25 years of age.

Again, I insist, teaching your child about money early on can help them avoid financial problems in the future. It won't necessarily guarantee them that, because each of your children has his or her own free will, but it will most certainly prepare them better. If you teach your children to save from the age of ten, for example, how much money could they have in the bank by the time they're ready for college? For life?

Another thing you can do with your children is to show them the financial statistics of the general population and what their average spending habits are like. Read a news article together that shows (preferably by using a graph) the large percentage of people who are in serious debt. Discuss with your children the poor financial habits of the majority of the population, and explain to them how someone can fall into debt.

Children love to be challenged and included in adult affairs. Money management is the perfect area to include them because children account for a large proportion of a family's expenses. They will love being included; they will want to teach their friends what they're learning, and they will rant and rave with excitement and pride over what they're accomplishing! Most importantly, they will learn something valuable that will serve them well for the rest of their lives. Develop their habits early on and have fun at it! Watch them grow and learn. Best of all, you'll have the satisfaction of knowing that *you* were the one who developed a training plan that was perfect for them! Who better to do this than their own parents?

Chapter 10

Why Have a Will?

Show me your ways, O LORD, teach me your paths. Psalm 25:4

The money we earn, spend, and invest can say a lot about our financial purity as a whole. Don't assume that because you are not a millionaire you do not have to manage your money because "you don't have enough to manage." *Au contraire*. If your finances are limited, this is all the more why you need to manage it wisely. I have heard people say time and time again, "Well, I am young and I don't make too much money, so what does it matter?" It matters a great deal! I cannot stress that enough.

Another thing people think about incorrectly is the need for having a Last Will and Testament. Handling your money wisely and having a will go hand in hand.

Whether you are eighteen or a hundred years old, I think everyone should have a will regardless of their age or their possessions. Do not use your age or your wealth status as an indicator of whether or not you need a will. Even in the Old Testament, having your house in order was a sign of godly conduct and behavior. If you are in the mindset that only rich people need a will, get in the habit of seeing things differently.

I have had many important debates with the youth of today on the importance of having a will. Having a will makes it possible for the people taking care of your affairs after you are gone to know what to do. Your will is a map of what to do, your personal wishes and desires on how to handle your affairs. If you do not tell them what to do, who will? Do you think they should have to guess as to what you would have wanted? Do they draw straws to see who gets your car? I don't think so. Most of the time fights and family dissension are the result of someone dying without a will.

It is important to tell your representatives what you want so they can carry out your wishes and desires effectively and without debate. That way you tell them this by having a written will.

I have seen many families, siblings to be precise, fight over land, homes, cars and other items all because neither of their parents had a will, did not think to create one, or thought it was not necessary. They probably thought their children would handle everything civilly. Well, that may be possible within some families, but that's not the case with all.

Here's a true story of a couple who did not have a will and what happened after their passing. I have the family's permission to share their story, but they wished to keep their names private, so we will call them the Sanchez family.

The Sanchez family lived (and some still do) in the exotic island of Puerto Rico where I am from. There were seven in the family, including their parents, who worked hard all their lives and acquired many items over the years. They had a lot of land, two houses, three cars, jewelry, cash on hand, and several bank accounts, but the parents died within a year of each other, and they passed away with no will or any written instructions as to how they wanted to disperse their properties and cash. Most certainly they wanted everything to go to their children, that was a given, but there were five of them, and lo and behold, the battles started.

This one wanted that, the other wanted something else, and on and on it went (you can only imagine). The arguments were intense, fierce, and sibling rivalry was strong. Other family members tried to mediate, but the arguments were so strong that they had to resort to legal and government intervention. This not only costs thousands of dollars, but the siblings' humiliation of not being able to resolve this among themselves was almost unbearable.

Well, they managed to divide the land up evenly, but one robbed the other of some land, and one sibling selfishly and quietly sold all their parent's belongings, including family heirlooms, and pocketed the money. This outraged the other siblings and has led to many fights and bitter arguments that are still going on to this day. Two of the five do not speak to each other, and there are still bitter arguments over the land. The legal part has been resolved, but the family is now divided. Three of the five siblings left the island and one of them has never returned.

There are secret rumors that one sibling dug into the other sibling's property in order to make his land bigger. They do not speak to each other. Respect is lost, and someone else has to mediate conversations between them if ever they need to communicate with one another.

You would think there would be more trust and amicability among them to handle these affairs quietly and fairly. But all too often, when people are left to fend for themselves, greed gets the better of them. Even the most respected adults can have trouble with their siblings in the absence of a will to determine who gets the various possessions left by their parents.

Because we never know the reactions or steps anyone can take, it is always good to have these matters settled well ahead of time with a written will. That way *you* get to make the decision as to how your properties will be distributed upon your passing. Never assume it is unnecessary to have a will. Never assume that just because you do not have grand wealth a will isn't needed, because it is. I have seen siblings and families fight over a $50,000 residence and a couple hundred dollars.

While we think this will not happen, we can never be sure. Properties and assets are a touchy subject, and there might be someone who wants more than his or her fair share. A simple will can settle all future arguments and provide a sort of safety net for the inheritors.

Not convinced you need a will? Let me share with you another case that hopefully will both shock you and perhaps motivate you to develop your will.

This situation involved another family of five siblings, who recently lost one of the parents. Neither parent had a will. As a couple they didn't have a joint will, either. Why, we will never know. I am also very sorry to say that each parent had a favorite child. They never mentioned it, but the siblings always knew who the favorites were.

A month after the passing of one of the parents, three of the siblings received an email from the living parent about the family property. The letter was long, but the point of the letter was to ask the three siblings to sign a letter of renouncement of the property. A letter of renouncement states that you are the child of your parents and you give up all right to any inheritance that is rightfully yours by birth. The reasoning was to let the "younger ones" have the property because they hadn't acquired anything of their own yet as they were still in school.

The letter also went on to say that the deceased parent had given up all of his rightful inheritance to his only brother, and because of this, they should do the same. He had signed a letter of renouncement and the letter was attached in the email. Now, imagine for a moment how the other siblings reading that email felt. The felt bad, humiliated, left out – in a word, they felt wronged. If the deceased parent wanted things to be left to the younger siblings then he should have specified that in a written and signed will to ensure that his wishes were carried out.

The three siblings refused to sign this letter of renouncement. They knew that would have been like giving up their birthright.

I share this story as a strong exhortation: Spare your children any possibility of having to sign a letter like that. If all the siblings agree to sign such a letter, then so be it, but doing so should not be asked of them. These issues can be touchy even for the strongest of families. If these issues are not handled properly, the result can be very hurtful, especially so soon after a parent's passing. Children feel close to their parents' property, and asking them to give up something so that only one or a few can benefit can (and most likely will) spark discord and cause division.

Fortunately, in this case, the siblings are still speaking to each other. However, the living parent no longer speaks to the three siblings who received the email. It is a sad situation, especially because now it is evident how the living parent has always felt.

Having a will can spare your child(ren) many problems. If you feel uncomfortable preparing one, do so for your children's sake. Even if you have one child, do it for that one child. If you promised someone something of yours when you pass, mention it in the will. Be clear and be specific. It can save many people much heartache and relationship issues, plus money.

Some states require you to have a will. If you do not, then your belongings pass to the state for them (strangers) to determine who gets what. That just doesn't sit well with me. I can take the time to prepare my will and update it on special life events. Take the time to make your will. It is quite simple to do, and with little or no money you can have one developed. You can type it up on your computer, sign it, have two witnesses sign it as well, and get it notarized to validate it.

A will makes a statement that you took the time to think about the future handling of your properties and affairs. It gives everyone else peace of mind; they will not have to think of these things because you will have already thought of them well ahead of time and you have left a map and a plan. There's that planning again!

Having a prepared will also saves money, not necessarily for you but for your children. If there is no will, and your children cannot decide among themselves how to handle your property, legal documents will need to be filed for an "intervention." Legal documents can vary, but one of them could be a form that documents who the children are.

This could cost a lot of legal fees, all of which your children or beneficiaries could have been spared if you had prepared a will. We all know the cost of legal fees can be atrocious, so think about that and help avoid getting your family into such matters because you did not want to develop a will.

Don't assume that a will can avoid any future arguments when you are gone. That is not the point. While it may aid in keeping the emotions calm and distribution of your assets and property fair, preparing the will is a decision you need to make. You need to develop your will yourself or with your spouse. You also need to have a will executor, an estate manager, or a Last Will and Testament representative. I recommend this be someone you trust who is outside the family, but the decision is yours. It just makes things easier and less emotional. Someone outside the family (someone you trust) can fairly take care of things for you and make sure all your wishes are carried out without getting emotionally involved.

Make your will and then enjoy the peace of mind it gives you to know that all-important task is done. Take the time to think everything through and state your wishes. Always remember to ask permission from the person you wish to be the executor of your will. Once you have their permission, then state this in the will.

Sometimes if a family member is in charge and they disagree with a request you've made, they may not carry it out. This is not necessarily bad; it is just that sometimes your requests are better handled by a non-family member. The decision is yours, but be sure to let the executor know how to access your will, meaning where they need to go to get it, or give them a copy. Leave this person instructions and a well thought out plan, including speeches, letters, and so forth. Arm your will executor with everything they will need to be successful in carrying out your wishes.

You might be thinking, *I want to do this, but how do I prepare my will?* It can be as simple or advanced as you like. You can write down on a piece of paper who you want to leave all your belongings to and sign it. Signing your will makes the document official. Otherwise, it is just a document that anyone could have written up.

You can have your lawyer prepare one for you and ensure that everything is covered. You can buy a template that has been prepared by lawyers and just type in your wishes. There are many options available to you.

Find one that you are comfortable with and can afford. You may not be able to pay a lawyer to draft one up for you, but you can probably find an affordable template in an office supply store. The important issue is that you prepare your will and update it regularly as needed.

Update your will every year or after every major life event like when a new baby is born, there is a new marriage in your family, illness, or the death of someone in the family who would have been a beneficiary or the executor, to name a few situations. You may also want to write a letter to someone and include it in your will package. You can also update your will anytime you like or whenever you feel it is necessary. The decision is yours.

Don't leave this to chance. You've worked hard for your property; make sure everything remains in order even after you are gone. Even if you are sure that your children can handle the matter themselves, prepare your will. You just never know.

You be the designator of who you want to bless with your belongings. What if you do not have children? The answer is the same! Prepare a will. Have your affairs in order.

Let's recap...

- A will is important to your family
- A will can save your family from division and dissention
- A will can save your family money by keeping them from having to establish legal documents
- A will shows you cared enough to think of your family
- A will provides clear instructions concerning your wishes
- A will is an important part of your financial purity portfolio

Having a will developed and established, meaning you have signed it and you have a will representative, is a part of your financial purity portfolio. It is a responsible thing to do. If I haven't convinced you yet, then pray about it and discuss it with people you trust. Get their opinions and ask them if they have a will themselves. It is an important step to take, but you need to feel right about it too.

If you do decide to prepare your will no matter what your age is, ask around for a good estate lawyer, if you choose to use one. Estate lawyers specialize in wills and estate management. If hiring a lawyer is not an option for you, then research online for will templates or look in your local office supply store for a will preparation package. You could also ask a friend if they have a template that worked well for them. You can simply state your will in plain layman's terms if you don't want it to sound like confusing "legalese." Just remember to sign your will, have two witnesses sign it, and then get it notarized, all of which will make it official.

Your age, marital status, and whether or not you have children or very many possessions should not be indicators of whether or not you need a will. Everyone needs to have a will so that their affairs are in order and their family can have a peace of mind.

Chapter 11

Your Financial Purity Portfolio

The Lord desires above all things that I may prosper and be in health, even as my soul prospers. 3 John 2

Look at your financial purity as a plan to get you to where you want to be in your finances, and because finances are linked to everything, your life. Many people all around the world come to the end of their life and realize they never achieved their dreams and desires because they never took the time to figure out what they wanted out of life. Because I value life, myself, and my parents, I need to make sure I make the best out of my life, because I will be here for a short period of time and I do not want to waste it.

Money is only one part of your life. Like anything else you watch over, manage, or take care of, your finances should be no exception. It takes great care, time, understanding, and attention to manage your finances wisely and effectively. If you neglect your finances, you will see the consequences of that neglect and the resulting negative impact on your life. Don't let your finances get to that point; instead, build your financial purity portfolio!

Now ... let's build your financial purity portfolio!

I recommend you use a binder in a color and design of your choice; they are sold anywhere and at reasonable prices. Next, use dividers for each one of the sections listed below and label them accordingly. If there is a section of your own you want to add, please do. The more organized and focused you make your portfolio, the more complete and structured your portfolio will be.

Here are the sections to label on the dividers in your financial purity portfolio binder:

Vision

Have you created your financial vision? If not, ponder how you envision your financial portfolio and life plan. Be specific. If you need help, pray about it and seek counsel. What areas do you want to improve? Where do you need to change? What are you doing well and thus can keep doing the same? What vision do you have for the next year? The next five years? Develop your vision, write it down, or type it up, and put a copy in your financial purity portfolio behind the divider labeled **Vision**.

Organization and Planning

Have you worked out a method for you and your family to achieve good financial organization and planning? Remember, there is a direct correlation between planning and organization, and saving time and money. Your organized method may be as simple as determining what days you and your family will perform specific duties. Take heart and make a plan. As I mentioned earlier, even the largest organizations including the military have extensive planning even for their everyday operations. Treat your life and that of your family with the same priority. You will get chores done faster and with much more ease. Develop your method, type it up, or write it up and place it behind the divider labeled **Organization and Planning**.

Tithing

Are you tithing ten percent of your income on a regular basis? Are you having money set aside from every paycheck for tithing and giving? Do you have fears and worries that you need to lift up to God and let go? Are you plugged into a church? Are you ready to let God bless you abundantly for your obedience and diligence to honor Him with everything you do? Label one of the dividers **Tithes,** and behind it insert a written plan for how and to which organization or church you plan to tithe. Don't leave this for later when you think you might have money available to give away. Tithing is not giving your money away – it is being intentional as to why and to whom you tithe. Tithing is about being diligent to God's way with money.

Prayer

Prayer is another important section in your financial purity portfolio and one you should not do without. Prayer helps to keep your mindset pure so that following God's commands is not a struggle but instead is a joy. Make a prayer list of all the areas you want to improve in, to strengthen, and to learn more about.

Saving

Saving consistently and diligently is another important section in your financial purity portfolio and one you cannot do without. Make a plan to set aside a portion of every paycheck. In this section of your binder insert a copy of your monthly bank savings account statements so that you can see at a glance how your savings are gradually increasing.

Credit report and credit score

Have you obtained a copy of your credit report recently? Do you know what your credit score is? We should all protect ourselves by getting a copy of our credit report a couple of times a year. Know what is on it, make sure it is accurate, and verify that all the accounts belong to you. Is your personal information correct? What do you need to work on? Fixing inaccurate information? Improving your score? Write up a plan and insert it behind the section divider labeled **Credit Report and Credit Score**. Remember, no one should know more about your credit score than you, so get familiar with it and stay on top of what you want to improve or change. You will not be able to change anything until you know what is showing on your credit report, so purchase a credit monitoring service and watch for any changes that may occur on your report.

Debt Management

Now that you have clarity on your credit report and credit scores, do you have clarity on your debt (if you have debt)? If you have paid off all your debt, congratulations! You can skip to the next section. But if you do have debt, get busy building a plan to pay it down and eventually pay it all off. It will take time, but the first step is to know what you are going to pay, when, and how much. Write up your plan and place it behind the section labeled **Debt Management**. Your debt management plan should also include how you are going to prepare a budget for the entire family to follow and how you plan to become resourceful in finding ways to pay down your debt. One of the key aspects of being resourceful involves removing any unnecessary spending from your life.

Teaching children

Do you have children? Are you working on a plan to teach your children about money, money management, and tithing? Teaching children early is the best way to prepare them for the future and help them become excellent money managers. One day they will have to manage their money on their own, so develop good habits in them at an early age. Get creative and help them learn different ways to make money. Instead of paying everything for them, why not give them the money and teach them to be good managers of it? Are there any tasks and chores you can give them so they can earn money? Make teaching children a part of your financial purity and look for different ways to stimulate their learning experience and enthusiasm.

Eliminating vices

Are there any vices you are spending your money on that you need to eliminate to keep the use of your money pure?

Last Will and Testament

The most misunderstood and neglected document is your Last Will and Testament. It does not matter what age you are or what your financial status is like, everyone should have a will prepared so that after you're gone, those managing your estate will have a clear direction and understanding as to how you want your estate to be distributed. Don't neglect taking care of this important document. Treat this part of your financial purity portfolio with the same importance and urgency as you do every other part.

Are there any other items you want to add to your portfolio? If so, add them along with your plan and follow through.

Your Financial Purity Portfolio

Your financial purity portfolio is now prepared. Use your binder to constantly understand, learn, change, improve, add, tweak, and teach as much as you can. You will now have a clear visual on where you stand and what you need to do to improve or develop your financial vision. Keep working at it, and don't neglect your portfolio just because you do not have great wealth. Develop it to achieve your vision and your own personal goals. Continue to be steadfast in prayer every day, and read the Bible to understand money according to the scriptures. There are many scriptures that support good money management, tithing, saving, and the importance of having a vision. Continue to ask God to provide you with guidance and wisdom in your finances so you can manage them well. Do not leave God out of your finances. When you include Him in this vital area of your life, He will bless you immeasurably for your faithfulness and the trust you put in His Word.

About the Author

Jessica V. Psalidas is the bestselling author of ***Everlasting Purity,* winner of 2008 Christian Choice Book Award.** Jessica is a cum laude graduate of the Inter-American University of San German in Puerto Rico with a degree in Business. She would later continue on to study **Faith Foundations** at the Institute for Christian Living with Charles Stanley and **The Way of the Master** at The School of Biblical Evangelism. Fueled with a passion to continue to study the Word of God and to serve the Lord, Jessica continues to have a daily commitment to focus on God's will for her life. Jessica has 17 years of experience working the business world and she coaches on the importance of purity. Jessica currently lives in Atlanta.

For more information please visit www.jessicapsalidas.com to sign up for mailings or to purchase her books. You may also find Jessica on Facebook at www.facebook.com/jessicapsalidas

Other books by Jessica V. Psalidas

EVERLASTING PURITY

The values we protect and stand by should also stand the test of time.

A practical and insightful book on purity. Everlasting Purity will help you understand the importance and value of purity and how to keep it in a world of weakening values and ever changing morals.

Everlasting Purity will help to empower you to become a women of godly excellence, and in doing so, to distinguish yourself in today's world!

Perfect for individual or group study.

Everlasting Purity is available at your local Christian bookstore or can be ordered from: www.JessicaPsalidas.com

Made in the USA
Monee, IL
08 November 2026

67382845R00155